SPEAK UP

LISTEN UP

SPEAK UP

GOD IS LISTENING

LISTEN UP

GOD IS SPEAKING

CHUCK DAVIS

**BEAUFORT
BOOKS**

SPEAK UP! LISTEN UP!

Library of Congress Cataloging–in–Publication Data on file.

ISBN: 9780825309359

For inquiries about volume orders, please contact:
Beaufort Books
27 West 20th Street, Suite 1102
New York, NY 10011
sales@beaufortbooks.com

Published in the United States by Beaufort Books
www.beaufortbooks.com

Distributed by Midpoint Trade Books,
a division of Independent Book Publishers
www.midpointtrade.com
www.ipgbook.com

Book Designed by Mark Karis
Printed in the United States of America

CONTENTS

PROLOGUE

A DEDICATION TO CARL TONNESSEN AND ALL THE INTERCESSORS

I AM A PRODUCT of God's workmanship. All glory goes to him.

Many faithful servants have partnered with God to invest in me as a son and servant of God. I cannot adequately express in words my gratitude for their investment. The roles that they have played have varied from teachers, to encouragers, to correctors, to supporters, to list a few. All of these were important, but I believe that those who took up the task of intercessory prayer on my behalf made the largest contribution. This book is written in dedication to those behind-the-scenes servants who prayed God's blessing into and God's covering over my life.

Even though women have carried the lion's share of these intercessions, I give special dedication to Carl Tonnessen. He was my first real mentor to apprentice me in prayer. Carl was a member of the first church I pastored beginning at the age of twenty-five. When Carl prayed you felt like God walked into the room. Carl had a rough, gravely prayer voice, and often prayed in King James English, which I think added a sense of gravitas to his prayer persona. He also repeatedly used phrases such as "tarrying in prayer," "taking hold of the horns of the altar," "calling down the unction of the Holy Spirit," "binding and loosing in Jesus's name," and "standing as a watchman on the wall," to name a few. He was a prayer technician. He also prayed God's Word. In essence, he was agreeing with God in prayer about the things that God had already declared as promises in his Word.

Beyond the form, when Carl prayed you knew that he had been in conversation with God before. He prayed with holy awe and simultaneous sense of friendship with God. I learned that this conversation had been developing for decades. Carl had set up a kneeler alongside a tree in the woods near his house and he spent hours there. Carl also dominated the volunteer list for mowing the church grass because he liked to walk the church property, praying for revival as he mowed the grass.

Carl tarried for decades in that small church, waiting for the revival to come. He had been talking with God and listening to God in prayer for years. He saw God move but not as fully as he would have wanted. He truly knew what the biblical writers meant in the notion of waiting on God. As a result, Carl was our church DP. Designated Prayer. Big event? Call the DP to the plate. Sickness? Get the guy closest to God to pray. Divine intervention needed? Carl.

I had an intellectual understanding of prayer as a young pastor. I could give testimony to answered prayer out of my own experience. I could theologize prayer. But I wanted more. I wanted to take hold of the horns of the altar like Carl. I wanted to call in God's victory for the people I served and to intercede for those still outside of relationship with God. So, I asked Carl to stop by the church on his way home from the ball-bearing factory a couple times a week. Our agenda: we would kneel at the couch in my pastor's study, and we would pray. At the same time, I instituted Wednesdays as a day of prayer and fasting at the church. Carl would be there at 4:00 a.m. with a couple other regulars and we prayed for a couple hours. The remainder of the day was filled with prayer gatherings and a desire in fasting to grow in our hunger for God.

I was apprenticed in the Carl Tonnessen School of Prayer.

Today, I honor Carl Tonnessen. He is part of my great cloud of witnesses who inspire me to run my leg of the race. I do so by praying. I do so by leading others in prayer. I do so by offering you this tool to grow in your prayer understanding and application.

1

AMANDA

*Prayer doesn't exist in some rarified spiritual world; it is part of the warp
and woof of our lives. Praying itself becomes a story.*

—PAUL E. MILLER[1]

IT WAS SEPTEMBER 21, 2013, 4:00 A.M. I heard the word
"Amanda" with a sense of urgency. I cannot tell you if that was
an audible voice or spoken within my inner heart. I had been
sound asleep. The previous evening, I had driven seven hours,
returning from a memorial service, to be a speaker at a retreat.
So, I was in a deep sleep.

I immediately thought of Amanda who attended the church
that I pastored. She and her husband Rubin were expecting their
first child. Our church is large enough that I lose contact with
individuals or families over a period of time. When you have
500 adults who make a local church their family and another

---

1   Miller, *A Praying Life*, p. 150

200 kids and teens, it is just not possible to keep up with the details of everyone's life. I wondered in my mind if Amanda had already had the baby or where she was at in the process of carrying the child, but even with my lack of detail I knew that I was to pray!

I am generally a sound sleeper. So, when I get an image of someone or hear a name in my sleep, I immediately assume that it is a call from God to pray.

It was dark and I did not want to disturb other people on the retreat, so I quietly got out of bed, knelt and prayed. For whatever reason, there was a special urgency because I prayed for over an hour. I may have prayed for other situations as well but Amanda was at the core.

Now how do I know that I prayed for over an hour? While I prayed, I had a sense that God wanted me to communicate with Amanda to tell her that God was watching over her and that whatever she was going through he wanted her to know that he was present. Because I sleep so soundly and tend to be moving at a fast pace during the day, I decided to send myself an e-mail from my phone so that I would remember to follow up after the retreat. Below is the e-mail.

Chuck Davis <chuck@stanwichchurch.org>   9/21/13 ⭐ ↩ ▾
to me ▾

Sent from my iPhone

Chuck Davis <chuck@stanwichchurch.org>   9/25/13 ⭐ ↩ ▾
to Amanda ▾

---------- Forwarded message ----------
From: Chuck Davis <chuck@stanwichchurch.org>
Date: Sat, Sep 21, 2013 at 5:08 AM
Subject: Amanda
To: Chuck Davis <chuck@stanwichchurch.org>

Sent from my iPhone

You will note in the screen save above that I forwarded it to Amanda four days later. I was delayed because of other ministry responsibilities, and then I was sick for two days. During that time, I discovered that she had delivered the baby over the weekend and there had been some complications. Thus, before I forwarded her a blank message with only her name in the subject line (the message shown above), I sent the following explanation so that it would make sense:

Congratulations Amanda and Rubin!

God had me in prayer for you over the weekend. I will explain.

I was at a retreat this weekend. I drove 7 hours to a funeral for one of my colleagues on Thursday night then back on Friday, arriving at the retreat late Friday night. I led the retreat all day Saturday, came back to two evening ministry pieces, all day Sunday and Monday ministry, and then sick these last two days. All that is important because in the flurry I did not send a message to you as intended.

I woke up in the middle of the night (Friday—really early Saturday) praying for you. I sent myself a message at 5:08 am with one word in the Subject line: Amanda. It was dark and I did not want to forget to let you know that I was praying at that time. I will forward it after sending this message. I wanted to explain before sending it so you would understand the context.

God was watching over you and called an intercessor to pray at the right time last Saturday. I pass this on to you at this time as testimony that He is watching over you now as you walk through complications.

Bless the Lord!

I had completed my assignment: prayer and encouragement. Then I received the following message from Amanda the next day:

From: Amanda Soosai
Date: September 26, 2013 at 10:29:25 PM EDT
To: Chuck Davis <chuck@stanwichchurch.org>
Subject: Re: Just got the news!

Hi, this is miraculous! Thanks for letting me know, it's so comforting to know that. I was in danger at that time. Thank God firstly that Abraham was supernaturally protected from all of the trouble and is a happy healthy boy. We'll have to discuss the whole story later when I'm fully recovered, but I went in for unplanned c-section at 12:40am Saturday, in good shape at that point. Baby was out fast at 1:04am, perfect. Then, things went downhill fast for me during the repairs. I was in serious condition after heavy blood loss. They were having trouble stabilizing me and had to give me some transfusions. I couldn't spend the first days with baby because I was so sick. But, with a lot of prayer and support we somehow made it through, and went home from hospital today! Life is finally getting back to some normalcy, but I'm still in a lot of pain and emotionally trying to process everything. Thank you so much for your prayers, there is no doubt that they made a difference. Will send out update to everyone in next few days.
Blessings,
Amanda

This story is especially meaningful to me on several levels. Amanda had come into vibrant relationship with God through Jesus Christ through the ministry of the church. Also, I had the privilege of dedicating little Abraham to the Lord several months after his birth. I felt at that moment that I was not only giving this child back to God as the true Owner and Caregiver but I was simultaneously giving his mother back to Abraham and his father. That rite of passage would have felt a lot different if it had only been Ruben and Abraham standing there.

Coincidence? I just happened to pray at the right time? I lack the faith to believe in such a random possibility.

Universal Energy? Really? I have to admit that I am a bit surprised that intelligent modern people can find this a better solution than a personal God who interacts with our world.

Mystery? Absolutely.

God didn't need my prayer. He allowed me to pray to

participate in His Restoration Project. Perhaps my prayer was to strengthen me in my faith pilgrimage? Maybe I am still so weak spiritually that I need sign posts pointing me to God? Or maybe my prayer was simply to encourage Amanda and Ruben in the midst of their pain, reminding them that life is not random and that they have a God who cares even when they are in the midst of life-threatening circumstances? As I process the many questions surrounding prayer, the words of Archbishop William Temple seem to align with my experience, "When I pray coincidences happen; when I don't pray there are fewer coincidences."

The story of Amanda is one of literally hundreds that I could personally tell. This does not mean that I do not have many unanswered questions about prayer. There have been times when I prayed just as diligently for other people or different situations but it did not turn out with the same happy results.

I have been disappointed in prayer many times.

But there have been other times when I cannot just write off the apparent interventions as mere coincidence, and these interventions push me to keep praying even though I do not understand completely.

Prayer is the first place where we partner with God.

Prayer is accessible to everyone in relationship with or seeking God. It is communication with the Commander and Chief of the Universe. And everyone is invited. Prayer is where we get our marching orders and then agree with God for his kingdom to break into our lives. It extends the footprint of the impact of our role in the kingdom of God to the extremities of the globe.

I invite you on a journey to increase your conversation with God.

Spend some reflection time around your own life experiences.

When have you experienced nudging similar to mine for Amanda that prompted you to act? Describe it in detail.

Did you immediately recognize it as God?

Are you unsure to this day that it might have been God?

What would it take for you to be convinced that God is a communicating God?

If you are still skeptical, would you be willing to pray the following prayer out loud?

God, your words recorded in the Bible say that if we seek you, we will find you. I am still unsure about this notion of conversation with you. But I have an open mind and I am willing to pursue the idea further. In this light, I pray a simple prayer: Speak. I am listening. If and when I hear from you, I make this commitment to find another person who has had a similar experience to explore it further. In your name, Amen.

If you are convinced that God is communicating, would you be willing to pray the following prayer out loud, and maybe with someone else who also believes?

Heavenly Father, I know that my attention toward you at this moment is because you have pursued me in love. You are the first mover. Jesus, I trust you as the Word and you said that your sheep would know your voice. I ask for a season in my life of greater alertness to your voice. Speak Lord, your servant is listening. In Jesus, Amen.

2

GAME PLAN: HOW TO USE THIS BOOK

You may be sure that the old Enemy is working by every means to frustrate your desire for good, and entice you away from every spiritual exercise of devotion ... to draw you away from holy reading and prayer.

−THOMAS À KEMPIS[1]

Pray as you can, not as you can't.

−DOM JOHN CHAPMAN[2]

BUT I'M NOT CARL.

I cannot even say that I have had an Amanda experience like you, Chuck.

Maybe those are the first thoughts in your mind?

As I think back on the story of Carl Tonnessen, to whom I dedicate this book, I realize that we can become so enamored

---

1   Kempis, *The Inner Life*, pp. 49–50

2   Coakley, *Dom John Chapman, O.S.B. (1865–1933)*, p. 245

with Carl's spiritual gift of intercession that we might miss God's everyday invitation for every one of us.

Prayer is not for experts alone.

Carl had a gift of intercession. Some people have a calling to spend more concentrated time with God in intense prayer. I will describe this later in the book, and I am grateful for those people. But if in our celebration of what these intercessors add to the world, you and I miss out on our opportunity to have conversation with God, we've missed an incredible privilege. Every person has access to God.

But I don't know how to pray!!

Prayer is like everything else in life. It develops with practice.

You did not walk the day you were born. You first learned the fine art of turning over. Then, you crawled. Then, you tried to stand up. Your first efforts likely involved someone or something propping you up. Then, one day you just stood there without a crutch. Then you plopped down. Then, another day, standing became a few steps. And lots of falls. Frustration. Then, more steps. Eventually, you wore your parents out as they tried to keep up with you.

You did the same with talking. In the beginning, you only cried or cooed your desires. You learned sounds by listening. You mimicked those sounds. After a long period of time, you added words. Words became phrases. You added grammar and syntax without knowing it. Phrases became sentences. Sentences became stories. Eventually, there were moments when you had to be told to be quiet.

My point: Becoming comfortable in prayer is a process.

It is a process in practice.

You will not learn to pray by merely reading about prayer.

Reading will give you fresh ideas and fill in your understanding. But the grammar and syntax of prayer are learned in talking and listening to God.

Will it be awkward at first? Absolutely.

It may even be frustrating. But it is worth the struggle. Max Lucado said, "Better to pray awkwardly than not at all."[3]

When you learned to talk, your speech was at first awkward, incomplete, and frustrating. You do not remember that now. You have become so comfortable and natural with forming ideas into sentences that you do not think about the mechanics of it. Conversation with God can have the same outcome. However, it will require you to practice.

So, here are my suggestions to you.

First, give yourself to the process. Eugene Peterson wrote a book entitled, *A Long Obedience in the Same Direction.* Use this book title as a mantra for your growing prayer life.

A long obedience in the same direction.

Commit to an extended time of growing in your conversation skills with God regardless of how awkward or frustrating it might be in the beginning. It could take a year or two—like walking and talking—but the freedom at the end is rewarding.

A.W. Tozer explained listening to God as a person's progression from hearing a sound of God walking in the garden, to the recognition of a voice that is not clear, to that moment that the voice is recognizable and even becomes an intelligible word.[4]

Second, give yourself to the practical exercises at the end of each chapter.

---

3   Lucado, *When God Whispers Your Name.*

4   Tozer, *The Pursuit of God.*

There is an old joke: *Young woman: "Sir, how do you get to Carnegie Hall?" Wise mature man: "Practice. Practice. Practice."* Everything worthwhile is worth the effort.

Excuse me as I go to another old piece of wisdom. I was raised with this adage on life: *If it is worth doing, it is worth doing well.* G.K. Chesterton turned the phrase a bit: *If it is worth doing, it is worth doing.*

Is there anything in life more valuable than an honest conversation with God?

In learning to talk as a toddler, you picked up non-verbal aspects of communication before verbal. This makes sense since communication theorists tell us that non-verbal is 90% of the message. Showing up to the conversation with God is 90% of the discipline. Turning toward him says, **let's talk!**

Third, get a plan. John Piper says it so well that I will leave this point to his wise words:

> [...] One of the main reasons so many of God's children don't have a significant life of prayer is not so much that we don't want to, but that we don't plan to. If you want to take a four-week vacation, you don't just get up one summer morning and say, "Hey, let's go today!" You won't have anything ready. You won't know where to go. Nothing has been planned.
>
> But that is how many of us treat prayer. We get up day after day and realize that significant times of prayer should be a part of our life, but nothing's ever ready. We don't know where to go. Nothing has been planned. No time. No place. No procedure. And we all know that the opposite of planning

is not a wonderful flow of deep, spontaneous experiences in prayer. The opposite of planning is the rut.

If you don't plan a vacation, you will probably stay home and watch TV. The natural, unplanned flow of spiritual life sinks to the lowest ebb of vitality. There is a race to be run and a fight to be fought. If you want renewal in your life of prayer, you must plan to see it.[5]

I wish it were more mysterious than this reality. We do what we value or love. Life is fast and moving. We need to form or nurture our values by planning and investing our time.

Fourth, when you are ready, take the risk of putting yourself with others who pray. Hear their prayer. Voice your prayer. And grow together.

Prayer is relatively easy for me because I grew up in a church where kids knelt with adults in prayer meeting. I learned the rhythm and structure of prayer even while I was learning the rhythm and structure of my maternal language. And I was encouraged to pray out, even when I did not have the vocabulary of prayer all figured out.

So that leads me to my fifth suggestion. If there are any children in your life, PLEASE begin praying with them. And I am talking about a conversation with God that goes a bit longer than a meal or bedtime prayer. Children, grandchildren, extended family of God children.

---

5   Piper, *Desiring God*, p. 182–183

As an adult, there are many things that I wish I had done as a child. Why? Because then these activities would be second nature to me.

For example, I can field a ground ball hit off a baseball bat without a blink. The only reason this is second nature to me is that I played pepper with my Dad just about every evening in the summer. Pepper is a game where you stand close to the batter, and he hits ground balls at your feet. It is quick and it is repetitive. Fielding a ground ball became a habit, a reflex. But it is a useless skill for me today. I do not play baseball or even want to.

It didn't hurt me to learn that discipline long ago. It was part of my development as a person. I learned discipline, team play, and leadership through sport. So, the disciplines gained in practice and repetition were useful in their time. However, today I wish I had invested that time in perfecting a golf shot. Golf would be much more useful at this age. Or to have learned to play a guitar. Again, more useful.

In my spiritual journey, my best investment of time, has been repetition in prayer. It is in my daily conversation with God that all fruitfulness in my life has followed. Everything else flows from this conversation. Maybe this is why of all the things the disciples could ask of Jesus, they requested him to teach them how to pray.

So, I encourage you in the process.

I want to challenge you to take the next step in your prayer life. I believe it is one of the most important investments that you can make in your life. To get a practical start, begin by doing an assessment.

Using a scale of 1–10 (10 highest), where is your prayer life?

It is good to have a real assessment of what is ahead of you. This way you will be able to celebrate the advances. And you can have a realistic developmental plan.

In your assessment, if you're a 2, don't try to be a 10. Set out on a plan to become a 3. Whatever level you are, just go up one more. How do you move from a 2 to a 3, or from a 7 to an 8, or even to begin as a 1?

Here are some questions to get you living into some new prayer space.

1. What do I need to adjust or be to take my prayer life up one level?

2. What areas of my life are creating too much noise and block out the hearing?
   - Relationships
   - Emotional wounds from past
   - Spiritual
   - Physical
   - Behaviors
   - Schedule

3. Of those areas, is there anything that I can adjust to remove some of the noise?

4. When and how am I going to adjust?

Pray. The appendices are filled with resources to get started. Begin by asking for God's help. Whatever He calls you to do, He will provide the resources to be successful.

Voice the following prayer:

Lord, I take you at your word. In the Bible, you are clearly depicted as a communicating God. You said things like—

if I would seek you, I would find you;

as one of your sheep I could know your voice;

that I could ask and expect to receive;

that I do not have to be anxious but can make my concerns known to you;

and that continuous prayer is a worthwhile goal.

So, as your child, I take my next step in prayer, trusting you. I do not have what it takes. But your Spirit can pray through me in ways that go beyond my capacity. In Jesus' name, Amen.

3

GOD WANTS TO TALK WITH YOU

To be a Christian and to pray are one and the same thing; it is a matter that cannot be left to our caprice. It is a need, a kind of breathing necessary to life.

—KARL BARTH[1]

When the Spirit has come to reside in someone, that person cannot stop praying; for the Spirit prays without ceasing in him. No matter if he is asleep or awake, prayer is going on in his heart all the time.

—ISAAC THE SYRIAN[2]

I GREW UP IN CLEVELAND, OHIO. I was born with a ball in my hand. I loved sports from the earliest age. And though I have not lived in Cleveland for almost forty years, I have remained a faithful supporter of Cleveland sports teams. For those of

---

1   Barth, *Prayer*, p. 15

2   Tan and Gregg, *Disciplines of the Holy Spirit*, p. 76

you who do not follow sports, you do not have any idea of the frustration of that fidelity.

Up until 2016, the previous championship won by a major professional sports team in Cleveland was 1964. Fifty-two years! The football team, the Browns, gave us that championship. I was only four years old at the time, so I only recall that championship through the recounting of my father and a vinyl record that was a recording of the play-by-play of the turning points and touchdowns in the game.

Gary Collins split right, Warfield to the left, Jim Brown lined up with Ernie Green in a T-formation in the backfield, Frank Ryan takes the snap and drops back to pass, Collins breaks open across the middle on a post route, touchdown!

I relived those championship moments over and over, waiting for the next one. We got close several times. But there was the interception, the fumble, the drive, the jump shot, the home run—all moments where championship was snatched from our hands.

Wait until next year.

Then in 2016, "next year" finally came, when LeBron James led the Cleveland Cavaliers to the championship of the National Basketball Association. Each game was heart-wrenching as the Cavs came back from a 3–1 game deficit to win the final series 4–3. This time "wait until next year" was snatched out of our hands, not the championship!

A few weeks after the championship, I was on a plane landing in Cleveland and the pilot announced over the intercom, "Welcome to Cleveland, the home of the world champion

Cleveland Cavaliers." That statement had a great ring to it even though I had not lived in Cleveland for nearly forty years.

WE WERE CHAMPIONS.

Do you notice the language that I have used throughout this description: *we* and *our*? As a fan of the team, I was emotionally engaged. I had deep loyalty. As much as I felt the disappointment in the years of waiting, I felt ownership in the victory.

Then, an event happened that was beyond my wildest dream. Somehow through a couple of my friends, word got to LeBron that I had been such a loyal fan over the years.

I EXPERIENCED THE UNIMAGINABLE.

My administrative assistant buzzed into my office phone and said that I had a caller on hold. It was LeBron James. I laughed. I thought it was one of my friends playing a joke on me.

I took the phone ready for a good laugh. But the minute I heard his voice, I realized it was not a joke. I had heard him interviewed multiple times. The intonation, cadence, and graciousness were easy to recognize. I proceeded to have a conversation with LeBron. It was one of the greatest earthly experiences that I have ever had.

Now if you are a sports fan, you can imagine with me how incredible it was to have this experience. If your interests are different—music, theater, politics, history, religion—with whom would you be amazed to have a conversation? Then put yourself in my shoes.

Now think about this fact. God wants to talk with you. He wants to have a conversation with you.

You are high on his list of appointments.

He wants to hear about your personal desires and your desires for your world. He not only wants to hear your voice he wants you to hear his voice. He wants you to experience his pleasure in you. He wants you to hear his desires for you and your world.

The Creator of the Universe.

The Sovereign Potentate over the movements of the Universe.

The Redeemer.

The Restorer.

The King

Now talking with LeBron, the king of basketball, is pretty spectacular. **But talking with the King of kings is another story.**

It is not just that talking with the King of kings is a possibility but that King of kings takes delight in talking with us. The conversation has been going on since before there was time. Father, Son and Holy Spirit in rich dialogue.

And he invites us into the conversation. In fact, he exhorts us into it. He is adamant about it. And his promise is that we would find him and partner with him in the movements of this world through the dialogue of prayer

This truth—**that God wants to converse with us**—may be the most important truth that we could get lodged in our souls.

Now back to LeBron. I made the whole story of our conversation up. He never called. We never talked. But I bet I got your attention!

However, the bit about God is not made up. It is true. I am talking with God right now even as I talk with you through this keyboard.

He and I have had many conversations. The recounting of

my conversation with God about Amanda was not made up. It happened just as I recounted. And that is only one of many conversations that I have had with God.

This book is written out of the overflow of those experiences. My life has been richly shaped by a biblically informed understanding of prayer and an ongoing practice of conversation with God.

My promise is this: If you will take up and explore this possibility for yourself, it will change everything about your existence.

PRACTICAL EXERCISE

Spend some time reflecting on what you think about talking to God. When you hear the word *prayer*, what words, concepts, or feelings strike you?

Have you ever thought *God has more important things to deal with than to speak with me?* Where does that thought come from? Sounds humble at first glance, but is it really humility to stand in contradiction to something that God clearly states?

Would you be willing to pray aloud this short prayer?

Lord, you have said in your Word that your sheep know your voice. I ask your forgiveness for not trusting you at your word. If there are wounded places in my soul that contribute to my sense of unworthiness to talk with you, please show me those places and lead me to healing. I reject any lie that might suggest that you do not have time or desire to be with me. I reclaim your Word promise of ears to hear. In Jesus, Amen.

4

"THERE IS SOMEONE HERE
WHO HAS A LEG INJURY"

"You're my child. My beloved. My pleasure." ... This is the message that blows quietly, sweetly through the whole Bible. ... It's so tender, so gentle, that it's easy to miss it blowing through my own little life story, with all its dramas and distractions.

—GREG PAUL[1]

Prayer is not conquering God's reluctance but laying hold of God's willingness.

—NEIL ANDERSON[2]

I WAS HEALED AS a nine-year-old boy of a severe fever. It was the type of fever where one minute I had a blanket on me because I

---

1   Paul, *Close Enough to Hear God Breathe*, p. 17

2   Anderson, *The Prayers of Jesus*, p. 99

was shivering from the fever and the next burning up in sweat. It was not my faith that corresponded with God's will to heal me that day. My parents had the faith to bring me to the elders of the church for prayer, following the injunction of James 5:14. God honored their obedience and faithfulness to take God's Word at face value. The elders anointed me with oil and prayed. I walked out of the church with no sign of fever.

A nine-year-old boy has no reason to manipulate the situation to create a God intervention. My response to any doubters or cynics after that event would have mimicked the response of the man born blind, who was healed by Jesus: "One thing I do know, that though I was blind, now I see."[3] For a nine-year-old it was as clear: "One thing I do know, that though I was burning up one moment and shaking the next with chills from a fever, now I am well and have energy to run around."

From that point in my life I did not need proof that God heals; I needed a theology to better understand his ministry of healing.

I can chronicle or give testimony to multiple other healings I have experienced or observed over the years—for me personally, for my family, and for people for whom I have prayed. But one of the times that I was healed remains outside the realm of normal. To explain the situation, I need to set the context.

In 2000, my family and I returned to America after a four-year term serving as missionaries in Mali. Three days after arriving in the States we met our extended family for a reunion at Bethany Beach, Delaware. At the time I was an avid runner,

---

3   John 9:25

running seven miles a day. Between 6:00–6:30 a.m. this God-providence day, I was running along Route 1, an area where hundreds of bikers and runners exercise every day. A driver fell asleep while traveling 50 mph and hit me from behind with his car. I was flipped into his windshield and was **thrown 30 feet up and 75 feet out**.

I landed in juniper bushes, semi-unconscious and pretty banged up. Today, as I type on my computer keyboard, I am reminded that I am a walking miracle, if not a living miracle. An interesting side note to this accident is that I landed in front of a sign right behind the juniper bushes that announced God's role in the accident: "The Preserve."

The first time I saw the police report below the reality of my preservation hit me with full force.

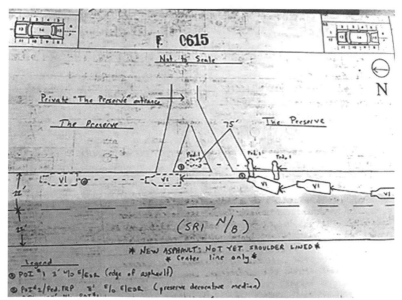

Police Accident Report: Chuck flying 75 feet in the air

God used multiple means to bring healing. There was extensive rehabilitation. There were even two moments of specific divine healing through the prayer of individuals in the first four months after the accident, but complete healing did not come for seven years. After seven years, I still had severe ankle problems. When I tried running again, my ankle could not take the pressure. Even when I sat in the car for an hour, I would get out of the car limping.

Then, the final installment of healing came, quite dramatically.

I had just begun my call to pastor a church in Connecticut. During those first months, I was aware of three severe situations for members of the church where they needed physical healing. There had been a few instances of healing in the church, a couple of them dramatic, but as we prayed fervently these three situations did not have the healing response we desired. At the same time, I became aware of a church in a neighboring town with a weekly healing service that was experiencing a special and regular grace-release of healing. As a result, I invited the three people to travel with me to the prayer service.

When we arrived at the healing service it was everything that I dislike about the stereotypical healing prayer ministry. The invited guest preacher and pray-er wore a white suit, with white shirt, white tie, and white shoes. He played the violin and sang. He spoke from a passage in the Letter to the Philippians but the message had nothing to do with the passage, nor did it reference healing. The service had all the appearance of the circus sideshow of the snake-handling traveling evangelist type.

However, I had come to know the pastor of the church, and I trusted him, so I pressed into the event. Through the whole service, I kept praying a prayer in the following vein, "Lord, I refuse to judge this visiting evangelist and his methods. You have obviously used him as a conduit of your blessing, or my friend would not have invited him. I refuse to box your way of working. I do not want any attitude in me to block what you want to do in the lives of the three people that I brought tonight." I prayed that same prayer over and over.

Then, the healing portion of the service began. A line was made for all those desiring healing to approach the healing "specialist" for prayer. Again, this is everything that I dislike in prayer spectacles. I prefer multiple prayer teams so that at the end of the gathering people point to God as Healer, and not to his representative.

But again, I fought a critical spirit, and I prayed not to judge. All three of my friends went forward for prayer and nothing tangible happened for them that night. But the oddest thing happened for me.

"THERE IS SOMEONE HERE WHO HAS A LEG INJURY."
While the line kept moving forward, the visiting evangelist suddenly stopped and blurted out, "There is someone here who has a leg injury." Knowing that I was fighting a critical or controlling spirit, you can imagine my first thought: *Yeah, there are over fifty people here that have leg injuries.*

Then the evangelist said the following, "This is strange. I pray generally for healing and God releases, but I am suddenly getting a message. There is someone here tonight who has a leg injury and God wants to heal you." To be honest, I was not immediately stricken with a sense of faith.

Then the evangelist got more specific. He stated, "This is

odd as I usually do not get this much instruction. You hurt your leg in a running accident. You have wanted to continue running but have not been able. God wants to heal you tonight."

Now I was fully implicated. He exposed my situation without knowing me. Immediately I knew that he had announced my healing. God was working dramatically outside my comfort zone and predetermined idea of how he should work. I went forward for prayer and anointing.

I have not had ankle problems since that time.

I am editing this testimony more than ten years after that evening of divine intervention, and I am physically whole. I have led three pilgrimages over the past three years where we walk 8–16 miles per day. No problem. Last week I hiked challenging terrain. No problem.

Why was I the one healed that night? I am clueless. To me, my injury was an inconvenience, but my friends' needs for healing were far more urgent, at least from what I could see in the natural. Likewise, God's healing cannot be due to my faith that evening. I spent the evening fighting unbelief and resisting judgment. I was not even there for my own healing. What I can say is this, "Once my ankle was a mess, and now it operates the way God originally designed."

Why tell this story in the beginning of a prayer book? I have found prayer to be a dynamic and mysterious practice. I cannot get around the fact that I have seen divine intervention to prayer. How could anyone with an honest, inquisitive view of my healing experience write it off as coincidence or self-generated well-being?

At the same time, I have been significantly disappointed at times when God did not respond to my prayer requests

in ways that made perfect sense to me.

What does this tell me?

It tells me that prayer is more than just asking and getting. God is doing something bigger and far richer in the conversation. Prayer is as much attitude as action, but attitude is formed in the regular action and the practice of prayer. So, I will say it again, I understand prayer *less* today than I did thirty-five years ago, but I pray *more* today than I did thirty-five years ago.

I invite you into this dynamic and mysterious journey.

PRACTICAL EXERCISE

Think through your own life pilgrimage. When have you experienced something that felt too eerie or mysterious to be written off as a coincidence? Was it a miracle? Have you talked to God about it? Questioned him? Thanked him? Asked him to help you with the remaining unbelief?

Ask someone who you trust if they have ever experienced what felt like a miraculous response to prayer. Do not critique their story, just listen.

Are you willing to share your experience with someone you trust? Maybe the same person who shared their story with you? Testimony unleashes faith.

5

ANOTHER BOOK ON PRAYER?

My persuasion is this: one's spiritual life will never rise above the practice of one's private prayer life.

−RICHARD BURR[1]

Every new Pentecost [Holy Spirit-led revival] has had its preparatory period of supplication. ... God has compelled his saints to seek Him at the throne of grace, so that every new advance might be so plainly due to His power that even the unbeliever might be constrained to confess, "Surely this is the finger of God."

−A.T. PIERSON[2]

REALLY? ANOTHER BOOK ON PRAYER? Doesn't the wisdom of the Preacher in Ecclesiastes warn us *"of the making of books there*

---

1   Burr, *Developing Your Secret Closet of Prayer*, p. 1

2   Pierson, *The New Acts of the Apostles*, p. 352–353

is no end"[3]? There are already so many books on prayer. Why another edition? Chuck, shouldn't you spend the time praying instead of speaking to others on the **why** and **how** of prayer?

Once a friend of mine was giving away a stack of books on the theme of prayer. When he was asked why, he responded, "It is time I stop reading about prayer and start praying." That insight is good for the already engaged and convinced. However, my experience tells me that most people idealize the notion of prayer, but few feel confident in the practice of it. And in my own experience, I need reminders to keep on.

I am simply adding the testimony of my life experience for those with whom I might have contact and influence. As a leader, I am called to a ministry of multiplication, not addition. I want to put my learned experiences in the hands of as many people as possible. Why?

Because my life has been transformed through prayer.

I have observed the movements of God in individuals, families, and communities as people have partnered with God in prayer.

Prayer is the most powerful activity available to humans on earth.

I am the product of God's faithfulness. It all begins with God, ends with God, and is sustained through the middle by God. It is in prayer that the realization of his abundance in my life has become so clear.

Over the course of this pilgrimage with God, he has used many people to shape me. Some have interceded for me, and

---

3   Ecclesiastes 12:12

others with me. I am indebted. I have seen the fruitfulness of God released through my ministry. I can tell you without hesitation that is a result of God's powerful right hand. Paul says it this way, "Some plant, some water, but it is God who brings the increase."[4]

I have led the people of God in vocational ministry for over thirty years, not by master planning or well-designed programming. I have introduced scores of the not-yet people of God to their Maker and Redeemer not by ingenious strategy.

I have prayed!

Yes, I have worked and mobilized the gifts of other people around me. And sometimes it was in the midst of prayer that strategy and program were unveiled to us. But at the core of it all has been prayer.

As a professor in a seminary, I often said to students, "If you are not going to pray, then do not go into vocational ministry." Then, I would leave an awkwardly long pause before saying, "No, really, I am not speaking in hyperbole here; if you are not going to pray, do yourself and the people of God a favor and do something else for your vocation."

Why?

Prayer is not preparation for ministry; prayer is the first work of ministry.

Prayer is ministry.

To attempt to be a representative of the kingdom of God and not pray is to put ourselves and the people we serve in danger. We do not need more powerless Christianity in our lives.

---

4   I Corinthians 3:7

We need God-saturated presence. We become alert and confident in that presence through consistent and long-term prayer.

Having said all of the above, I want to make a point that this book is not only for people in vocational ministry. I believe every Christ follower is called into ministry. I have watched the members of the local congregations that I led partner with God in life-transforming prayer. It may have been a team leader on the trade floor, or a stay-at-home parent over the sink, or a school teacher in the classroom, or a steamfitter on the construction site—all were making a difference by working hard and praying even harder.

Who I am today has been shaped and prayed into existence by many unpaid ministers (at least, unpaid in an earthly, monetary sense). I am the product of praying saints. And I serve in a community of prayers who are being transformed inwardly, living faith outwardly, and partnering with God to change the world, through action coupled with prayer.

So, this book **is** for everyone. I especially believe this book can help to empower the novice or the person on the outside looking in. Even if you are experienced in prayer ministry, this book can be a fresh surge to a larger partnership with God for the unleashing of his kingdom in this world.

I believe that we are in a spiritual war. There is a lot at stake for our families, our churches, our communities, our nation, our world, and for ourselves. We have become soft in the West. Terminology like "spiritual warfare" offends our ideas of a comfortable life, but we cannot read the Bible without seeing the backdrop of spiritual conflict:

Creation was barely alive, and enmity enters the story.[5]

Redemption was unfurled, and darkness threatened to overcome.[6]

We may not like the terminology of warfare, but that does not make warfare any less real. We are fighting for the soul of all that really matters.

My belief is that God is shaping his people to be overcomers in that war. In Revelation, it says of the faithful that "they have conquered by the blood of the Lamb and by the word of their testimony."[7] I add my testimony of prayer to the ongoing story of God's people overcoming.

So, here is my advice on how to continue: read, pray, read, pray, read, pray, and so on. I believe the best way to grow as a Christ-follower and ambassador is a continuous cycle of learning and doing. It is the orthodoxy-orthopraxis cycle. Orthodoxy is *right thinking*. We need information to enlarge our knowledge. Orthopraxis is *right practice* or right doing. Information without application falls short. Thus, the best way to benefit from this book is to do the practical exercises offered throughout.

Jesus applied this principle to the Word of God in a parable about two builders. One built his life on a solid foundation of rock; the other built on a suspect foundation of sifting sand. When storms came, the sand was washed away from the

---

5   Genesis 3

6   John 1

7   Revelation 12:11

foundation, and the building came tumbling down. The house built on the rock, however, stood strong through the storm. The implication of the parable is that the person who builds her life on the Word of God builds on a rock that will make her stable when life's tempests threaten well-being. Jesus then interpreted his parable with this notion: a person who builds on the rock not only hears the Word (orthodoxy) but does the Word (orthopraxis).

Likewise, the best way to grow in prayer is a cycle of having our minds stretched, plied, or even renewed with knowledge, while putting the insights into practice. So, read and practice. For some of you the concepts will not be new. I have read the Bible dozens of times. Yet each time I open the pages of the Bible, I rediscover aspects of my faith journey that are not new but inspire me to stay on course. For others of you, the concepts will be new. Either way, a renewed mind (orthodoxy) and scuffed-up knees (orthopraxis) will unleash the kingdom of God around you as you partner with God.

Read, pray, read, pray, read, pray, read, pray, read, pray...

PRACTICAL EXERCISE

I have found it important in prayer to find a strategy that works for me. If I wait for prayer to happen, it won't. It is in the discipline of regularly scheduled time with the Lord that I have developed a listening ear to pray continuously.

I decided a long time ago that this means I must begin my day with prayer. Get up, get coffee, get my Bible and journal, and allow caffeine to quicken my body while the Spirit quickens my soul. Some mornings I don't feel like it, but the determined pattern gets me there.

I also know that I cannot have other things on my mind—I am too easily distracted. No phone, no texts, no email, no news before I sit with the Lord.

When I am traveling or have an early meeting, I do not have the same luxury at times. This does not throw me off. It is the long practice that keeps me in focus. But my soul knows when it is thirsty, and sometimes in those irregular times I will get up earlier, even in the middle of the night, because a well-saturated soul is essential to healthy living.

You need to find your pattern. The following questions are important:

1. What 15–60 minutes will you make your regular "I am here to talk, Lord" time?

2. Where will you go to have quiet and uninterrupted time?

3. What will be your pattern? Knowing what you are going to do going into the time saves mental drifting.

Once these are determined, give yourself a month of consistent practice to see if it makes a difference in the richness of your prayer life.

PART I

QUESTIONS SWIRLING
AROUND PRAYER

I GREW UP PRAYING. My parents prayed—for meals, before trips, in times of need. They did not just pray at church—we prayed at home, in a restaurant, alongside the road, in the homes of friends. I was also part of a church where the practice of prayer was embedded in the life of the church gatherings. Many times, we would kneel as an entire church body between pews or around circles of metal chairs in the church basement. I became comfortable in praying spontaneously by hearing thousands of prayers and offering up my prayers in between those of others.

I recognize now that I grew up as a privileged child. Accessibility to God was never questioned. I learned early that I was praying to the Father (Jesus's model prayer: Our Father). I learned early that I had access to the Father through Jesus.

Jesus told his disciples, you have yet to pray in my name[1] and to ask anything in his name.[2] As a Christ-follower, I had access to God through the name of Jesus. I learned early that it was the Holy Spirit who was praying through me as I conversed with God.[3] Prayer began as a formula, but over time I came to the place where I felt freedom to dialogue with all three members of the Trinity.

The act of praying is not as comfortable for everyone, especially the act of praying out loud with other people. Not everyone grows up in a community that fosters dialogue with God as I experienced as a child. Many of us grow up with a church experience where others prayed for us; it was clergy activity and specialized. Others of us pass through childhood without a church experience. Nevertheless, although it is easier to grow up doing something naturally, I have watched people transform to feel a freedom to pray, even without the childhood experience.

I have been with literally dozens of people when they all of a sudden found the courage to pray out loud amidst a group of people for the first time. Often it was in a time of crisis, especially for someone they loved. The urgency, the desperation for intervention took all nervousness away, or the familiarity of people around them made the setting safe to wade into new waters. Then I have watched those people take off.

This book is for both groups of God-pursuers. Those who

---

1   John 16:24

2   John 14:14

3   Ephesians 6:18; Jude 1:20

feel comfortable praying and those just starting to grow into it. Even though I have prayed for years, I occasionally need a boost in my prayer life. I will read a new prayer book, or even a classic that I have read before, and my prayer imagination will be inspired.

If you are just beginning in prayer, the more you understand, the more freedom you will feel to grow into a daily dialogue with God. To help you grow into this freedom, I will begin by addressing some of the big questions surrounding the practice of prayer: faith, a communicating God, mystery in prayer, disappointment, and the discipline of waiting.

6

THE ISSUE OF FAITH: PROVE IT!

God's "response" to our prayers is not a charade. He does not pretend that he is answering our prayer when he is only doing what he was going to do anyway. Our requests really do make a difference in what God does or does not do. The idea that everything would happen exactly as it does regardless of whether we pray … makes prayer psychologically impossible, replacing it with dead ritual at best.

—DALLAS WILLARD[1]

The future is not set in stone. The prayers we pray and the decisions we make in the here and now have a direct, line-of-sight effect on what does—or does not—happen down the line. Because God responds.

—JOHN MARK COMER[2]

1   Willard, *The Divine Conspiracy*, p. 244

2   Comer, *God has a Name*, p. 65 [kindle]

THE BIG QUESTION IS **"Does prayer really make a difference?"**
We live in a world that is cynical and skeptical about the things of God and faith. We want proof that prayer really works. In reality, the average person has decided that prayer does not work. Thus, even stories like the situation of me praying in the early morning for Amanda are assigned a naturalistic explanation.

The challenge is that the efficacy of prayer cannot be proven from a scientific perspective. Modern science has attempted to use double blind tests to prove that prayer makes a difference. Every so often a study is released in a contemporary journal or magazine where a scientific observation has been made. In a hospital, a group of patients will be prayed for, while another group of patients will not be prayed for, with researchers making observations of the healing process or lack thereof. Often a test group is included in which the patients are being prayed for and do not know it. Including this group is intended to remove the potential for self-generated healing caused by the positive emotional energy created by a sense of being cared for. The conclusion to these scientific studies is often striking in its affirmation of prayer.

My response to those studies may surprise some people. Even with the data that shows that people tend to get well more regularly with prayer, even when they do not know they are being prayed for, **those tests do not prove anything to me.**

Prayer, as all faith issues, is not "scientifically" provable. Faith issues are mysterious and trans-rational. God is not rational. This does not mean that he is irrational. My simple point is that God's ways are not my ways, and the more I know him, the more mysterious he becomes and yet more real and dependable. God is trans-rational.

Prayer as a conversation with him must also be trans-rational.

The Bible embraces this mystery. God is Sovereign, unchangeable, yet he relents to the pleading of his people in prayer. He is a pursuing God in His love, yet tells us to persevere in prayer with an intensity that almost suggests that he is an unwilling responder.

The psalmists complain in prayer. Abraham barters in prayer. The prophets punctuate the urgency of their prayer with bizarre actions, all under the direction of God. The early disciples refused to move without prayer. The apostle Paul captures the mystery of prayer by speaking of the impact of unintelligible groans:

> Likewise the Spirit helps us in our weakness. For we do not know what to pray for as we ought, but the Spirit himself intercedes for us with **groanings** too deep for words.[3]

Add to this the prayer gift of tongues, which does not always come with cognitive understanding or meaning. Groans and prayer tongues are neither rational nor irrational—they are trans-rational. So, there is always the underlying question of mystery to prayer that keeps us humble, holding lightly our ideas on prayer.

---

3   Romans 8:26

NATURALISTIC WORLDVIEW

Beneath the question **"Does prayer really make a difference?"** are a whole set of worldview assumptions.

The naturalistic philosophers look at prayer as wishful coincidence. Karl Marx viewed all religion in general as the "opium of the masses."[4] He believed it was a way of anesthetising one from the random pain of life, and thus, prayer was a delayed response in a denial of reality. Immanuel Kant called prayer "a fit of madness, talking to oneself, superstitious illusion; excuse not to fulfill moral duty."[5]

The truth of the matter is that if one has decided not to believe in the possibility of communication with the Divine, or eliminated the Divine all together, there is no proof that can be given that will convince a person that certain unexplainable experiences of life can be connected to prayer.

At the core of a naturalistic worldview are two starting points. One begins with a complete denial of a Divine Creator or Sovereign. This denial is called atheism. However, some people find that the world is too brilliant and complicated to be attributed solely to random combustion. Even Albert Einstein noted that there had to be an intelligence or spirit superior to man to account for the laws of the universe in which he had placed his faith. As a result, many who hold to creative design but who do not know what to do with the "inconsistencies" embedded in the mystery of prayer have chosen a worldview that restricts divine intervention in the day-to-day. This is

---

4   Marx, *A Contribution to the Critique of Hegel's Philosophy of Right*

5   Kant, "Religion" in *Lectures on Ethics*, p. 194–198

called Deism. Many of the early American fathers, schooled in Enlightenment thinking, were Deists.

Deism holds to the notion of a closed universe. In a closed universe, God created the universe and our world. The order is explainable by an Intelligent Designer or Creator. However, in this worldview, the Creator created the world as a self-contained system that operates according to rules, what we call the laws of nature. Even though the world we live in has brokenness, the Creator does not enter in to interfere with natural processes. This leaves room for a belief in God (first mover and creator) but eliminates the idea of miracles as well as the work of prayer as a means for calling for Divine intervention.

The Deistic worldview helps the person who struggles with the times that God does not answer prayer in the way we would desire. Suffering, then, is not random but the result of certain rules within the creative order, with which God does not interfere.

I do not find this philosophy satisfying simply because of the reality of miracles. A miracle by definition is an intervention that cannot be explained by natural processes.

I have experienced miracles: immediate healings that cannot be explained by medical science; connections that changed lives dramatically that are too purposeful to be explained as randomness; unexplainable shifts in weather and natural order. I cannot muster the intellectual dishonesty to explain those events away. Thus, I am left with a mystery in relation to the "inconsistent" results of prayer. But it is illogical to me to move from mystery to eliminating God's engagement in our world.

The challenge of prayer is not the appearance of miracles.

The challenge is found in the times when an all-powerful and all-loving God seems to withhold a miracle in response to what appears to be sincere, persevering, faith-filled, and what seems like God-honoring prayer. I will address this more later.

THE SOVEREIGNTY OF GOD

Beneath the question **"Does prayer really make a difference?"** are a whole set of theological assumptions as well. The discussion of the effect of prayer has not only been a part of the discourse of philosophical naturalists; at times, it creeps into our theological discussions in the community of faith.

Theologically, there is the question of how prayer intersects with the Providence or the Sovereignty of God. One response to prayer that I have heard in light of the Sovereignty of God is "God is going to do what he wants anyhow, so prayer does not make a difference." Even the sayings of Jesus can be used to substantiate this perspective on prayer:

> And when you pray, do not heap up empty phrases as the Gentiles do, for they think that they will be heard for their many words. Do not be like them, for your Father knows what you need before you ask him.[6]

I have heard people say in response to this saying of Jesus, "See God already knows what you need, so why pray?" The problem is that this way of thinking takes Jesus's words out of context. Jesus was addressing a misunderstanding about the

---

6   Matthew 6:7–8

method of prayer, not the efficacy of prayer. After giving his warning, he then goes on to teach the followers **how** to pray. Jesus would not teach his disciples how to pray if it was a useless activity.

I have yet to find an adequate response to the question of Sovereignty and the role of prayer. Again, I find this discussion falls into the category of mystery. However, I do not need to be able to explain prayer to be convinced that I should pray. I do not need to be able to explain the mysteries of prayer to know that it is important to what God is doing in our world.

There are two primary reasons to pray. First, the Bible not only invites us to pray, it commands us to pray. Obedience is the first motivation for prayer. God would not tell me to do something if it were not important. God is not trivial in his dealing with us as his children. The second reason to pray is even more convincing: Jesus prayed. The example of Jesus ends up being my most compelling reason for me to pray. There are at least 45 scripture passages where Jesus prays or references prayer.

The gospel of Luke especially captures Jesus as getting his direction from the Father in prayer. At each great transition moment, for his life and ministry, Luke shows Jesus in prayer. Consider the following examples from Jesus's own life and teaching, just from the gospel of Luke:

- He regularly created space in his own life to pray.[7]

- He prayed during his baptism.[8]

- He prayed for guidance before calling the apostles.[9]

- He prayed before the Father revealed his identity to Peter and before Jesus revealed to his disciples that he would be crucified.[10]

- He prayed at the Transfiguration.[11]

- He prayed in his own agony in the garden.[12]

- He prayed from the cross.[13]

- He called the Temple a house of prayer.[14]

- He told his followers that spiritual harvest was connected to

---

7   Luke 5:16; 9:18

8   Luke 3:21

9   Luke 6:12

10   Luke 9:18

11   Luke 9:29

12   Luke 22:40–45

13   Luke 22:34,46

14   Luke 19:46

prayer;[15] that prayer was a space to experience the glory of God;[16] to pray so as not to fall into temptation;[17] to not give up or lose heart by staying engaged in prayer;[18] and even that they were to pray for their enemies.[19]

Given Jesus' prioritization and personal investment in prayer, it is no wonder that the disciples asked Jesus to teach them how to pray.[20]

The disciples knew experientially and intuitively that Jesus operated out of the flow of his relationship with the Father. That relationship was fostered in prayer. Think about it: of all the things they could have asked Jesus to teach them, they requested teaching on prayer. Why not more spectacular requests? Lord, teach us to do miracles. Lord, teach us to walk on water. Lord, teach us to multiply bread, heal the sick, cast out demons, or raise the dead. The disciples asked the Lord to teach them how to pray because they recognized that prayer was at the foundation of all that he did to demonstrate the arrival of the kingdom.

Once we move beyond the useless attempts to scientifically prove prayer or the contrived theological constructs to explain away "unanswered" prayer, and embrace the mystery of God's

---

15   Luke 10:2

16   Luke 9:29

17   Luke 22:46

18   Luke 18:1

19   Luke 6:8

20   Luke 11

invitation to join him in his restoration project through prayer, we can then build the fundamental blocks of prayer.

Prayer is first and foremost an attitude and action rooted in faith. There is an element of mystery to it that causes me to be suspect of any teaching or notion that creates formulas of transaction. *If I pray this, God owes me that.* That is manipulation of God. At the same time, I refuse theological notions that overextend the Sovereignty of God to the point that prayer has no impact in God's unfolding plan in the Restoration Project.

Prayer is not just a psychological device to settle my heart to receive what God had planned anyhow. When I read the Bible, I see a clear relational partnership between God and his people. That relationship and partnership is maintained through a conversation: prayer.

I will never coerce God to give me what is outside of his will. But at the same time, I may miss some of his *along-the-way* blessings for me by not asking in prayer. If this were not true, why would Jesus say, "You have not because you ask not"?[21]

So given the uncertainty, why do I pray? Jesus prayed and the Bible instructs me to do likewise. And though I cannot explain prayer and all the mysteries surrounding the efficacy of prayer (at least as how I interpret efficacy), I still pray. Prayer is an odd mix of trust, obedience, faith, abandonment, and desperation! Most importantly, it is the conversational space and dialogue of an ongoing relationship with God.

---

21   James 4:2

Which of the above objections—philosophical or theological—have you found challenging to your own expectations in prayer?

What life experiences have fueled or demotivated your prayer initiative?

Are you willing to pray to God for adjustment to any of the deficits noted above?

Pray something like this ...

Lord, I have allowed certain philosophical or theological ideas block my conversation with you. I invite you to open the eyes of my heart to know your hopeful inheritance in my life, an inheritance that includes hearing your voice. In Jesus, Amen.

Lord, my personality and life experiences have made me uncomfortable or suspicious of a conversation with you. I ask you to overcome any place that is set up against my ongoing conversation with you. In Jesus, Amen.

7

DOES GOD REALLY SPEAK TODAY?

The whole Bible supports the idea. God is speaking. Not God spoke, but God is speaking. He is by His nature continuously articulate. He fills the world with His speaking Voice ... The tragedy is that our eternal welfare depends upon our hearing, and we have trained our ears not to hear.

A.W. TOZER[1]

"Dear God, I think about you sometimes even when I am not praying."

—THE PRAYER OF ELLIOTT, A LITTLE BOY

EUGENE PETERSON STATES BOLDLY, "The fundamental conviction of our faith is not so much that God *is*, as that God *speaks*."[2] If prayer is a dialogue, then the fundamental question before us is "Does God speak today?" If we begin with a conviction that God is not speaking today then we will not expect a dynamic

---

1   Tozer, *Pursuing God*, p. 73, 77

2   Eugene Peterson, First and Second Samuel, Kindle edition loc 667 of 5870.

process of conversation.

Cessationist theologies have proposed that God communicated directly to individuals in the past (in biblical times and in the early days of the apostolic church) but after the establishment of the Canon of his Word, direct communication was no longer necessary. These theologians began with an assumption that God does not speak today and then developed an interpretation for the Bible that supported their idea. The initial intention with this idea was to elevate the role of Scripture. However, as with many of our theological notions, this idea was pushed to its illogical extreme. The assumption was that the Bible, given by God, was such a perfect standard that God did not need to add any other communication. Let's examine the cessationist claim further:

Part 1—The Bible a perfect standard. TRUE.

Part 2—God did not need to add any other communication. FALSE.

It is not a matter of need but of desire. God speaks. He likes to communicate.

I agree with the desire to elevate Scripture. The Scriptures are God-breathed and the final standard for life and practice. Though I believe that all of God's communication must accord with the final standard of his written Word, I do not believe that he has quit giving messages beyond that Word. What do we do with notions like guidance, direction, calling, divine assignments, if God is not speaking a fresh word daily?

We will be weakened in our prayer life if we cannot get to

the point of hearing God. God will use his Word in that process, but he will go beyond his Word if we allow our ears to be tuned to his voice. He could not have told me to pray for Amanda (Chapter 1) with his Word alone. For one thing, I do not believe that the name Amanda occurs in the Bible. Moreover, how would the speaker have known to call me out for prayer for the healing of my leg (Chapter 4)?

My experiences confirm that God is speaking. There are days when I get messages from God all day long. *Call this person. Go visit this person. Pray for this person.* Impressions. I have come to trust those impressions. It is amazing how many times on the other end of the phone, the person will say, "Your call is timely," or "It feels like you have been reading my mail." **I am unwilling to give these occurrences away to the god of random or nebulous "Universal Energy."** I find it takes a lot more faith to to explain away these "coincidences" than to believe that there is a divine presence behind the impressions. So, why would we theologically give such occurrences away to a predetermined theology of God's silence?

My experience clearly shapes my beliefs, and my beliefs have become reinforced by my experiences. Some might call this a circular argument, but it is no less circular than deciding (whether philosophically or theologically) that God does not speak and then interpreting life from that perspective by basically explaining away the mystery of timely interventions. I prefer a life of engagement with God and being available for his assignments. As a result, my ear has been tuned expectantly to his voice in the quietness of a daily set-aside time of conversation.

SO HOW DOES GOD SPEAK TODAY?

The follow-up question is then **"How does God speak today?"**
Hebrews 1:1–2 states:

> *In the past God spoke to our forefathers through the prophets at*
> *many times and in **various ways**, but in these last days he has*
> *spoken to us by his Son …*

A quick reading of this verse might cause one to think that
the various ways God communicated in the past stopped. This
is not the point of the writer of Hebrews. Rather, the writer
emphasizes the clarity, fulfillment, and excellence of the Word
as spoken in incarnate form of Jesus. Jesus was the "radiance
of the glory of God and the exact imprint of his nature."[3] Jesus
was the most brilliant expression of God's Word.

God as Spirit, and not incarnationally present, was only
experienced prior to Jesus in manifestation. A voice from heaven.
A cloud. A pillar of fire. Writing on a wall.

Now in the flesh. God was right in front of our eyes.
Speaking in the local dialect.

As John wrote in his letter to the church, "That which from
the beginning, which we have heard, which we have seen, which
we looked upon and have touched with our hands…"[4]

Even the perfection of the Word in Jesus did not mean that
God no longer needed to communicate in various ways. Jesus
was the ultimate expression of God but not the only expression.

---

3   Hebrews 1:3

4   I John 1:1

Thus, our starting point for developing a practical theology and practice of hearing God begins with the most common ways that he spoke in the accounts of scripture: "in the past."

God spoke to his people in the scriptures in the following ways: with audible words, through signs, through a phenomenon, through a phenomenon with a voice, through supernatural messengers (angels), through impressions ("still small voice"), through human messengers such as prophets, through dreams, and through his Word.

In summary, God speaks in many different ways.

Since we are to live by the standard presented in the Bible, it makes sense to me that God would continue to communicate in these same manners today. The advantage we have over most of his people recorded in the biblical text is that we have the Bible in our hands as a guide to be sure that the messages we receive line up with what he has already stated through the written Word.

Since we are to live in the Way of Jesus, it makes sense to me that we would communicate with the Father in the same way that Jesus did. Jesus said, "Those who believe in me will also do the works that I do."[5] John tells multiple stories of Jesus getting his commands from the Father. Jesus offers this explanation: "The Father has given me what to say and what to speak ... I say as the Father has told me."[6]

As with all disciplines in life, learning to commune with God can start off rather awkwardly. In the beginning, we

---

5   John 14:12

6   John 12:49–50

have to devote ourselves to prayer.[7] Over time, the process of prayer—the dialogue and the listening—becomes more familiar.

In the beginning, it seems hard to pray for five minutes. Eventually we arrive at a place where prayer is so comfortable and becomes so important to our life that we cannot get enough time to pray. However, reaching this point takes time and practice. The long-term result will be a 24/7 interaction—on the spot, minute-by-minute, continuous conversation with God. As one author notes, "Prayer isn't primarily words; it's primarily a place, an attitude, a stance. That's why Paul could say 'pray always' and 'pray unceasingly.'"[8]

PRACTICAL EXERCISES

Think through the following questions. Then find a trusted friend or two, and talk through the questions. Try to enter into them with an open mind. You are looking at life experience and not taking a stance of judgment.

What faith traditions have influenced your prayer life? Do you find the notion of God speaking fresh words to people today easy or challenging?

What is your feeling or reaction when someone says, "God told me?"

If you remain a skeptic, what would it take for you to move from skeptic to surprised conversation? Are you willing to ask God to surprise you? And if you are willing to ask, are you willing to question your own beliefs and assumptions if he does surprise you?

---

7   Colossians 4:2

8   Rohr, *Everything Belongs*, p. 81

Pray the following prayer or something like it.

God, my experience has caused me to question your interactive and fresh communication in the every day. I want to be an honest agnostic, so I am willing to hold my assumptions loosely. I welcome your surprise communications in my life. If and when I sense a breakthrough, give me the courage to act on what I think that I am hearing. And give me the integrity to live out of a new belief system. In the name of Jesus, Amen.

8

DOES GOD REALLY WANT TO
SPEAK TO ME TODAY?

Here is the most amazing feature of grace; although God has no need of us, being complete within himself, he earnestly desires that we be on speaking terms with him.

—CALVIN MILLER[1]

Failure to pray will harden us and deafen us to God's presence. Prayer trains us to hear God's presence in our world, and all the people who silently walk into the rooms of our lives, and all the words not spoken. Our prayerlessness is not about how busy we are or about all our good intentions gone wrong. It is about the state of all calloused, hard of hearing hearts. The irony is that the thing we are registering is the only cure for the ailment: prayer.

—LONNI COLLINS PRATT AND FR. DANIEL HOMAN[2]

1   Miller, *The Path of Celtic Prayer*, p. 28

2   Pratt and Homan, *The Benedict Way*, p. 41

I HAVE HAD PEOPLE SAY TO ME, "I would pray but I think God has more important things to take care of in the universe than hear my request." This objection sounds humble at first take, but it is really quite arrogant, or at least is false humility, because it is pride in the form of self-deprecation. Why would God tell us to pray if he didn't want to talk to us? This type of objection also reduces prayer to a *transaction-only mode*, failing to see prayer as the communication mechanism for my ongoing relationship with God.

Others say to me, "God speaks to you that way, Chuck, but not to me." My response is to wonder if it is a matter of God not speaking—or us not listening. My conviction is that God desires to communicate with all people. I think many people agree with this statement in principle. They would agree that God does speak; he speaks to others. However, those same people often do not expect God to communicate personally with them. My point is so important that I am going to state it again: I believe that God wants to be in active communication with everyone—**that includes you.**

Jesus said it this way: "My sheep know my voice."[3] The image of sheep is metaphor, but knowing his voice is not. The only reason that it would be important for us to know the Shepherd's voice is to be engaged in communication. Thus, we need to deal with the beliefs, attitudes, or experiences of our lives that have predisposed us not to expect God to speak.

Maybe you feel blocked in your conversation with God? Or maybe you feel stalled? Maybe you were never given permission

---

3   John 10:27

to pursue this aspect of your relationship with God? When I tell my stories of dialoguing with God, people will ask, "Why doesn't God speak to me like that?" The following steps can reveal or unlock the next level of the dialogue.

ATTITUDE AND ACTION STEPS TO HEARING GOD

1. Realize that God is a communicating God who wants to disclose himself. (Genesis 3)

2. Believe that he will speak to you. (John 10:1-16)

3. Desire to hear from Him. (Hebrews 11:6)

4. Ask Him to speak to you. (Matthew 7:11)

5. Spend time in the Word. (Hebrews 4:12)

6. Be willing to act on what you hear. (I Samuel 3)

7. Record what you hear. (Psalm 63:6; Habakkuk 2:2)

8. Get a coach or mentor. (I Kings 19:21)

After the belief that God does not speak today, I think that our own, personal insecurity can be the greatest blocking point to hearing from God. Second to that is a fear that we might not like what we sense we are hearing from God.

First, believe that God will speak to you. Let me state it more strongly. God **wants** to speak with you. As I described earlier, there are people who think that God speaks today, just not to them. There is an underlying question of personal worth: why would God speak to me? If you are in that place, you need to break that false agreement off of your life. Your worth is rooted in Jesus.

Communication is more God's desire than yours as he can only be known through his self-revelation; he is Spirit. A relationship with God depends on his initiating communication. But, as with a phone call, initiating the call is only the beginning. Someone else needs to answer their phone to make it a conversation.

Etch this into your beliefs: God loves you and wants to spend time with you. The pure joy of conversation with the living God is a gift beyond description. Besides, the life benefits that accompany prayer are out of this world. Allow God to love you by believing that he wants to spend time with you and talk with you. If that seems too hard to believe, find someone who can help you go to the wounded places that block you from a mutual and loving relationship with God.

I recently have been reflecting a lot on the notion of God's pleasure. The idea of his love wedged into my soul long ago. I have no doubt that I am loved. I know there is nothing I can do to add to that love or subtract from it. God's love is unchanging. Whether it is his Old Testament *hesed* (lovingkindness or faithful love) or his New Testament *agape* (unconditional love), I feel saturated and safe.

But there is also this element of his pleasure.

The Father declared his love over Jesus at the beginning of

his ministry. At the same time, he declared his pleasure: *"This is my beloved son, in whom I am well pleased."*[4] We might want to say, "but that was Jesus." He was the Son in a unique sense. However, the psalmists remind us that this pleasure is not simply for the Son; it is for all sons and daughters of the Lord:

> But the L ORD takes pleasure in those who fear him.[5]

> For the L ORD takes pleasure in his people … .[6]

Nothing can separate me from God's love—but I can affect his sense of pleasure.

My relationship with my adult children gives me insight into this reality. They cannot do anything to change my love toward them. I love them regardless of their performance. I love them in spite of how they treat me or respond to me. However, my sense of pleasure *for* them—more than pleasure *in* them—is related to how I see them flourishing in their lives. I derive pleasure from their pleasure, especially when that pleasure is rooted in God's good design for them.

God wants to speak with you. In fact, it gives him incredible pleasure to dialogue with you.

---

4   Matthew 3:17

5   Psalm 147:11

6   Psalm 149:4

God said that if you seek me, you will find me.[7]

God said that if we draw near to him, he will draw near to us.[8]

God said listen to my voice.[9]

God would not have made himself so accessible if his intent was to remain distant. The pursuit begins with him, but the response grows in desire with us.

Finally, our growing in the flow of communication is linked to **our willingness to act on what he speaks.** If we are honest, we often ask God for direction but we simply want him to confirm what we already want or desire to hear. So, we continue to miss his message. In the scriptures, we see periods where the hearing of God's word was limited because the people were not acting on what God was saying.

This is classically portrayed in the story of Samuel.[10] God spoke audibly to him in the night when he was a boy serving in the temple. "Samuel." It was so clear that each time Samuel went to Eli the priest to find out what he wanted. After the third time, Eli instructed Samuel to respond the next time with these words, "Speak for your servant is listening." And God spoke.

What a great moment! In this scripture, we are told that the

---

7   Jeremiah 29:13

8   James 4:8

9   Jeremiah 11:4

10   I Samuel 3

word of the Lord had been rare for hundreds of years. That rarity was not initiated by God but self-inflicted by the people who had wandered from him. Basically, they quit doing what he had already told them. This was true especially among the priests. Over time, their ears became blocked or dulled to God's voice.

The word to Samuel was an historical, breakthrough moment. He would eventually be given the secrets of God for Israel. It was to be a season of fresh communication. However, the reception of the initial message put young Samuel in an awkward place. He had received a hard word about what was to happen to the family of Eli, his mentor. When Eli asked Samuel what the Lord had said, Samuel was hesitant to pass the message on. But Eli demanded to know.

When the hard message was shared, the old priest honored Samuel's faithfulness. God began revealing the secrets for his people through the prophet Samuel. Eli and the boy prophet both learned a fresh lesson that day. As we are faithful with what we hear from God, both the easy and the hard assignments, he sends us more and more. I call it the Samuel Principle: as we are faithful with the small messages, we will then be ready for greater messages.

ONE FINAL EXHORTATION

Even when we get past bad theologies or predetermined ideas about ourselves, we then face the challenge of a lifestyle that makes us miss God's regular communication. Recommitment to the belief that God speaks, and the fact that he speaks to us, will require some life changes to transform our ongoing dialogue with God.

We have so much noise in our day-to-day existence that

God's voice is simply drowned out. The noise is both internal, through emotional dissonance, and external, through social interference. Our physical space is invaded with the noise of constant media and technical devices. I am bombarded daily with bells and whistles that tell me I have a text message waiting, a tweet response, a new Facebook post, or an important email message in my inbox. It is interesting; I talk less on my phone today, and yet my mental space is invaded more than ever. Some of those pieces of communication are important, but the constant flow and volume can make it harder for me to listen.

We are a distracted people!

We need to make choices throughout the day to purposefully remove noise from our lives. The missing ingredients for hearing from God in contemporary society are Solitude and Silence! As we create space for solitude and silence, our ability to receive instructions in day-to-day life will be strengthened.

Now, we all can have runaway thoughts, so there is an element of discernment in determining what is my own thought and what is God's intervening impression. That discernment is also fostered in the consistency of time with God in his Word. I cannot expect to hear God's daily word, which is so subjective, when his written Word, which is less subjective, is not part of my life.

Growing in the disciplines of solitude and silence to tune our ears becomes important in moments where the noise cannot be shut out. For example, at the moment of spiritual warfare all types of rumblings will occur; darkness will use spiritual noise as a means of creating fear or confusion. As we move in the flow of what God is saying, we will be able to step into this confusion as a calming presence in Christ because we will have the ability to hear God's battle instructions. In the words of Isaiah the prophet, "You will hear a voice behind you saying, Walk in it."[11]

Jesus is the perfect example of one who created the time and space to tune his ear to the Father. The gospel of John describes his battle strategy: I go where the Father is going, I do what the Father is doing, I only say what the Father is saying. How did Jesus know each of these? His spiritual ear was tuned in solitude. The gospel of Luke tells us that Jesus often went off to solitary places.[12] If Jesus needed it, how much more do I need it? Solitude creates the space for me to be attentive to God's manifest presence. Henri Nouwen says it well, "I was able to embrace solitude ... as a royal road to God's presence."[13]

The generations following mine have it even harder. They grew up with electronic devices as appendages. My observation is that they are rarely in community space, focused and engaged with what is going on immediately around them, because they are lost in a world "out there." Thus, the invitation of God, "Be still and know that I am God,"[14] becomes even more important in the day in which we live. If we do not take this challenge to "be still" seriously, our ability for intimacy will be weakened. Without determined effort and consecrated space for solitude and quietness with God, we will not tune our ears to his regular messages to us.

---

11   Isaiah 30:21

12   Luke 5:16, 9:18

13   Nouwen, *Discernment: Reading the Signs of Daily Life*, p.10

14   Psalm 46:10

If we are going to be serious about developing a conversational relationship with God, it will mean that we will need to take the noise of our lives seriously. If you find yourself in constant mental conversations with others, then you might need a good session of inner healing to discover why those voices occupy your mental space and to get relief from that emotional noise.

And every one of us will need to take the social noise into account. We are so addicted to it, we might benefit from a social media fast, purposefully finding space so that our lives are not filled with external and interrupting noise. I have a friend, who decided with her husband, that they along with their three active children and teens would include a separation from social media on the Sabbath (a time they have decided will be Saturday sundown through Sunday sundown) for the sake of removing the social clutter from their lives. That regular break might be all that we need. However, it may be possible that we may need more extended times of fasting to break our bondage to noise.

Does God speak? His communication is our only way of knowing of his existence. Does God speak today? My experience and others' suggest YES. Does God speak to you today? That is a question that will take some change in our lives if we really desire to hear from him.

PRACTICAL EXERCISES

Review the list from page 58—Attitude and Action Steps to Hearing God. Where do you need help? Who around you can help you find direction to take the next step?

I have prepared a short prayer for each of the steps.

1. Realize that God is a communicating God who wants to reveal Himself.

> *Lord, I am willing to accept that you are a communicating God. The Bible itself describes you this way. Would you allow me to see fresh expressions of your self-revealing character as I read the Word? In Jesus, Amen.*

2. Believe that he will speak to you.

> *Lord, I renounce any sense of false pride rooted in self-deprecation that would make me think that you would not communicate with me. I ask for your healing and closing of the places where those thoughts came to me. I ask for Holy Spirit-ignited faith to expect to hear from you. In Jesus, Amen.*

3. Desire to hear from him.

   and

4. Ask him to speak to you.

> *Lord, I want to hear your voice. Speak, your servant is listening. In Jesus, Amen.*

5. Spend time in the Word.

Lord, I commit to be more attentive to you in your Word. I ask for your help in finding a regular time and rhythm of reading and hearing your word. As I read it, will you open the eyes of my heart see your message to me in that Word. In Jesus, Amen.

6. Be willing to act on what you hear.

Lord, I do not want to be only a hearer of your Word. I want to be a doer of your Word. As you speak, give me courage to act on what you say. In Jesus, Amen.

7. Record what you hear.

Lord, as I write down or type what I think I hear you say, I ask for recall to return to that word when it comes into fruition at a later time. I ask that this simple exercise will increase my confidence to respond to what you are saying. In Jesus, Amen.

8. Get a coach or mentor.

Lord, would you direct me to someone who has had experience of talking with you so that I can learn more. I renounce a spirit of independence in my pilgrimage with you. Grant me community to grow in this practice of speaking to you and hearing from you. In Jesus, Amen.

You may be further along in the discipleship of prayer than that which the prayers above describe. If that is the case, I celebrate God's good work in you. And I offer this prayer to you.

Lord, many of your children do not have a sense of confidence to converse with you. I am grateful that you took that barrier away from me. I want to help others find the freedom that I have found in my conversation with you. Will you direct me to some people that I might invest in for their benefit. In Jesus, Amen.

9

THE MEANS OF RELATIONSHIP
WITH GOD

Our private and public prayer is our chief expression of our relation to God.

—ANDREW MURRAY[1]

There is a great beauty in the movement of the soul as it forsakes its alienation and inability to hear, know, and be friends with God, and comes into the position of listening, illumination, and union with Him. There is a splendid simplicity to it.

—LEANNE PAYNE[2]

TO FULLY ENTER INTO an understanding on prayer, we must realize that prayer is first and foremost about the development

---

1   Murray, *Waiting on God*, p. 22

2   Payne, *Listening Prayer*, p. 167

of our relationship with God. Reducing prayer to a transaction of getting what we want (intercession or supplication) or warring against darkness (spiritual warfare prayer) takes the element of relationship building out of the practice. Prayer is the initial place, attitude, or activity where we foster relationship with God.

Stated simply, prayer is first **keeping company with God.**

If I begin with prayer as transaction, it will feel like a duty rather than a privilege. However, if I start with prayer as an invitation to relationship with the Living God, it is far more compelling. Think about it: we are invited into God's throne room for discussions, conversations. If a famous human requested the same, I would not hesitate to clear my calendar to have the opportunity.

The God of the Universe offers us such an opportunity.

George MacDonald captures the value of experiencing the presence of God in prayer, over and against the notion of prayer as a transaction:

> The one who prays and does not faint will come to recognize that to talk with God is more than to have all prayers granted—that is the end of all prayer.[3]

This relationship-building aspect of prayer can be a bit obscure because God is Spirit. We find relationship building challenging with other humans who are physically present. Thus, it is even more challenging and takes more deliberation to build relationship with God, who is Spirit.

---

3   MacDonald, "Man's Difficulty Concerning Prayer"

Added to this tension is that He is Abba Father (familiar and close) and at the same time the Almighty (totally Other and beyond our best imagination). It takes time and practice to learn how to communicate with royalty.

I have an acquaintance who has dined with the Queen of England. Dining with a queen was not like a meal in our own dining room. There was specific dress, specific terminology, specific rules on when to talk to the person to your right and then when to turn to the left. There is a culture of social rules around that communication, all initiated by the Queen.

How much more for God? It is all initiated by him. In fact, apart from his self-revelation to us, our best imaginations and efforts can't get us to an understanding of who he is or how to communicate with him. We need time in dialogue to develop the familiarity and recognition of voice. But if we will dedicate ourselves to the process, prayer will move from transaction to transformation as we learn to saturate ourselves in the manifest and revealed presence of God.

Thus, prayer is the conversation place where we develop an intimate relationship with God. Charles Kraft notes the foundational element of intimacy to the activity of prayer:

> I believe the most important of the things we refer to as prayer is what I term practicing intimacy. This is the activity of simply being with God, inviting him to come and be present with us. ... I think this is what Jesus usually did when he spent the night with the Father.[4]

---

4   Kraft, *Communication Theory for Christian Witness*, p.7

Prayer begins with a growing intimacy with God. Intimacy is created through presence and openness, which requires dedicated space and time in conversation. This means that we will need to develop the process speaking and listening in order to truly develop our prayer lives.

PRAYER IS A TWO-WAY DIALOGUE

Many people begin with a one-way conversation in prayer—us talking to God—and never moving on to the more robust form of dialogue. We have not been as disciplined to develop the listening aspect of prayer. Charles Kraft writes:

> We often spend the whole of our solitude with God talking, with little or none of it spent listening. A pastor friend of mine pictures the average prayer as a telephone conversation where one person talks and talks and then, before the other can say anything, hangs up the phone. When we practice God's presence by relaxing with him, we allow him opportunity to express himself to us in a way that doesn't happen when we are engaged in talking.[5]

Listening is a great American weak spot to begin with. We do not attentively listen to people who are present in the flesh. Then when we add all of the noises and movements of our contemporary lives, we find ourselves in a vacuum of silence or solitude to develop ears that hear God's voice. Since we do not do this well with other humans, the challenge of listening to God, who is

---

5   Kraft, *Communication Theory for Christian Witness*, p.7–8

Spirit, becomes even more challenging. If God's most common means of speaking is in a "still small voice," then it is challenging to be focused and quiet long enough to discern that voice.

I am not sure that this is just a problem of our contemporary times. The ancients of the Bible had the same problem as it was often at night, or in the wilderness, or in purposeful solitary places that God was most profoundly heard. It has just become more challenging with ever more external noise.

Mother Theresa described her prayer life in the following manner:

> My secret is a very simple one, I pray.
> Prayer is simply talking to God.
> He speaks to us; we listen.
> We speak to him; he listens.
> A two-way process: speaking and listening.[6]

It would be easy for us to say, "Yeah, but that was Mother Theresa." She is exceptional. Interestingly, in her final memoirs she talks openly about her moments of doubt and questioning of God. Even for people who walk with great fortitude and in the Jesus way, it takes faith and perseverance to develop this prayer conversation.

This again pushes us into the mystery of prayer. I have been actively praying for many years. Honestly, I can explain the mystery of prayer less today than any time in my life, but even so, I pray more than ever.

---

6   Yancey, *Prayer,* p. 65

Why? Prayer is the place and space of being most attentive to God in relationship. Interestingly, I also pray more and more with the Bible open. Maybe it is in the intersection of God's written Word and my availability that his freshly spoken words come into tune. The written Word is as objective[7] as we can get and provides a good basis for his more subjective day-to-day word.

Along with an open Bible, I have found that confidence in the dialogue with God has come for me by journaling. I write out some of my prayers in the morning. I write out the impressions that I am getting from his Word. I record notions that pop into my mind. This allows me to confirm messages that are coming through and to begin to trust what I sense I am hearing from God. When the same word or notion comes to me from different sources or directions, I don't second-guess what I am hearing because I can confirm it in my journal.

I can give an example from my conversation with the Lord

---

7   Please note that I say that "the Word is as objective as we can get." It is still a subjective process. We cannot help but read the Bible through our own worldview, assumptions, personality types, experiences, and will. Beyond that, God's Word is so rich and there are so many hermeneutical tools to understanding its meaning that the reading is a constant mining of new insights. The more I see, the more I know. And the more I know, the more I see. But truthfully, we can easily bend the Word to say what it never intended. This is the reason that it is important to read the Bible in community; a community that searches the whole biblical text with an historical and orthodox understanding of how the church has consistently interpreted the most basic and essential aspects of the Christian faith. I mention examples of people making the Word say something that is contrary to what the Word says in its most simple and clear reading. Often this is done in the name of *sola scriptura*—that is, we only have a theology from Scripture. However, our faith is established in historical certainties that lead to profound mysteries that keep our discipleship and witness humble.

just this morning as I prepared for my day in quiet time. I began by writing out a prayer. It was spontaneous writing. Here is the prayer from my journal:

> *Lord, I press into you. My mind starts to race into "to do." I stop to wait on you, to become. Pushing in. I remember the word that was sent by email to me yesterday: "Be watchful, stand firm in the faith, act like men, be strong" (I Corinthians 16:13). Lord, I can only do this as I press into you—abiding!! I am physically tired. Pressing in to refuel. Taking a hold of your life. In Jesus, Amen.*

As part of my spiritual discipline, I read the Bible in sequential sections, allowing the Word to go deeply into my soul. My text for this morning in the chronology of reading was I John 2:18–29. The exhortation to abide occurs five times in that passage of Scripture. The three most prominent calls to abide: abide in the Son, abide in the Father, and abide in him. Because of my opening prayer and the confirmation of the Word, I finished my meditation and chewing on the Word with a short prayer,

> *Lord, I press in to you to abide but also to hear more about abiding. In Jesus, Amen.*

Immediately, my eyes went to a book on the table next to my study chair where I pray. I heard in my inner being, "Read Chapter 4." I opened the book, and it was filled with discussion of the Apostle Paul's life of prayer and devotion, as the basis for life and ministry. The author challenged our common reaction to think of Paul "basically as a thinker and doer rather than as a prayer and a passionate lover of God." Paul came to know the resurrected Christ initially through a strong revelation of light and voice—an experience. He then spent a period of time searching the Hebrew Scriptures (his Bible and Jesus' Bible) to make sense of his experience. Then, he did kingdom things— more experience. I doubt he put his Bible down between those experiences. He grew in his experiential knowing of Christ by abiding. To borrow from my prayer: waiting, pushing in, pressing in, being watchful.

In those moments of quiet, God had tied together several thoughts of prayer, Word, and insights from another author, to give me a fresh word for the day. In that moment, I immediately set aside my normal plan of devotional activity with God—as stated, I have a pattern that I follow daily. The Word for the morning was to put all that aside and spend time abiding, or waiting on the Lord. Some might call it saturating in his presence. For me it was simply a conversation or dialogue.

I was then able to use the insights of that time with God to help several people that day. I realize this example is not spectacular—no flashes of names like with Amanda, no advance knowledge of a situation or person to care for, no supernatural intervention. But this account is important, as it is partly describing my relationship building process with God. I have learned to be alert to the flashes through the consistent rhythm of daily talks with God. However, that alertness has been cultivated in the mundane, everyday, un-amazing, conversation with him.

TIPS FOR INCREASING CONCENTRATION FOR
DIALOGUE WITH GOD:

1. Prayer and Movement: I am an active person. Sitting still
   can sometimes make the attention needed for conversation with God difficult. I have found walking while I
   pray to be a great energy release. I am not referring to
   the practice of prayer walking (see in Chapter 28). I am
   talking about strolling in conversation. I have done this
   both in beautiful settings that ignite my creative side or
   even in walking slowly around the exterior of our house
   or the church.

2. Prayer and "To Do" Lists: I am not always able to stroll
   and pray, thus I have learned some ways to keep my
   focus. Inevitably, when I sit down to pray, my mind
   gets bombarded with things that I need to do or people
   that I need to reach out to. I keep a pad next to me that
   is separate from my prayer journaling. I can write those
   flash thoughts down, and thus I am not worried that I
   will forget to follow-up later. It keeps my mind free to
   stay engaged in the dialogue with the Lord.

3. Praying Out Loud: This is where it is helpful to have a
   designated and private space to pray. God can hear my
   thoughts. However, it is easy for me to slowly bleed over
   from a prayer thought to a worry, or even rabbit trail to
   other areas. When that happens, I do not beat myself up. I
   just acknowledge to the Lord that I got distracted and that
   I am back. Praying out loud can make the rabbit trails less
   invasive. However, since it is dialogue, it is good to stop
   talking out loud and to listen as part of the conversation.

4. Prayer Plan or Model: I have found it helpful to have a plan, map, or overall flow to my established prayer times. The structure serves as a skeleton that holds the larger prayer time together. I have had various patterns over the years so they can change for freshness of application. My present structure has the following categories: Missionaries and Mission Settings, Family, Personal Fruitfulness, Church, Friends. Since I have a number of repeat prayer requests over a longer season in each of these categories, I have an established plan to my prayer time that gives structure while leaving space for Holy Spirit direction.

Once my teenage daughter asked me the following question after having seen God specifically direct us as a family: "Dad, you are always hearing from God. How do you know it is his voice?" Great question! I responded with this image. "When I call home and you pick up the phone, and I simply say 'Hey,' how do you know it is me?" Her response: "I know your voice, Dad." I believe that we learn God's voice by spending consistent time with him.

My conviction is that God desires to communicate with all people in this manner. Desmond Tutu, archbishop in South Africa, stated the same conviction:

Dear Child of God, all of us are meant to be contemplatives. ... Each one of us is meant to have the space inside where we can hear God's voice. ... As we take time to be still and to be in God's presence, the qualities of God are transferred to us.[8]

---

8 Tutu, *God has a Dream*, p. 99–100

Once again, I believe that God wants to be in active communication with everyone—**and that includes you.** I have taken the time to write this book to bless you in that conversation and relationship building. I cannot speak strongly enough of the liberation of an active and daily relationship with God, over and against a distant appeasing of a mechanical and distant deity. The only way to learn how to pray is to do it. So, your practice and conversation over these next days and weeks will be key.

PRACTICAL EXERCISES

What needs to change in your life to build up the conversation with God?

Do you have an established place and time for the conversation? If not, why not establish that now?

Do you have a plan? If not, why not establish that now?

Which of the tips above might take you to the next stage of your prayer life?

Here is a prayer for you, no matter where you find yourself in your development as a pray-er:

Lord, I want a fresh season of hearing from you. I offer my ears to you anew. Remove all blocks or unhealthy filters by the healing blood of Jesus. Recharge them by your Spirit that I would distinctively know the tone and cadence of your voice. In Jesus, Amen.

10

WAITING ON GOD

In prayer it is better to have a heart without words than words without a heart.

−JOHN BUNYAN[1]

God aims to exalt Himself by working for those who wait for Him. Prayer is the essential activity of waiting for God—acknowledging our helplessness and His power, calling upon Him for help, seeking His counsel. ... God is not looking for people to work for Him, so much as He is looking for people who will let Him work for them.

−JOHN PIPER[2]

THERE IS MUCH TO LEARN from those who have gone before us. I learned to pray by being with people of prayer. I have also gained much from observing the practice and perspective of distant mentors.

---

1   Bunyan, *The Poetry of John Bunyan*

2   Piper, *Desiring God*, p. 170–171

The psalmists are mentors. They wrote out their prayers. These recitations became the expressions of praise and supplication to God, and even complaint, for the larger faith community. They express an open, uncalculated, and unguarded conversation with God.

God in his Sovereignty hovered over the psalmists by his Spirit to make these prayers part of his inspired Word. You cannot go wrong praying the Word. When I am at a loss for how to pray, I like to pray those ancient prayers today or build off of them for more current prayers.

I also have mentors from more recent history. Hudson Taylor and Andrew Murray have mentored me in the practice of prayer. I never met the psalmists who lived millennia before I was born. Likewise, Taylor lived over fifty years before I was born and Murray nearly one hundred. But as I read the writings of each of these faith-filled people, I am instructed and inspired in my own prayer journey.

One practice I learned from these mentors was to "wait on God." At first glance, waiting seems like a passive activity. But the sense of waiting that the psalmists describe is an active expectancy of God's intervention. Some from the nineteenth-century holiness movement, such as Andrew Murray, would write about tarrying in prayer.

Waiting is not something we are accustomed to as contemporary people. We are an "instant" society. We take now and pay later. We have lost a sense of delayed gratification in the mundane world. This clearly leaks into our spiritual pilgrimage.

In prayer, the act of waiting is important to God's greater purposes for us. Waiting enlarges our capacity to trust. Waiting creates expectancy for the unveiling of God's promises. In the

God-breathed words of the prophet Isaiah, "God … acts for those who wait on him."[3] If our sense of comfort were his greatest concern, all of our desires would be his instant command. He is far more interested in us becoming overcomers than being comfortable.

Whereas the noise of life is a detriment to listening in prayer, our bias toward action can be a detriment to waiting in prayer. Many of us have heard this admonition: "Don't just stand there, do something!" The children of God who want to move in the flow of his plan might begin in the reverse, "Don't just do something, stand there!" Thomas Merton writes, "In the active life as everywhere else, the better part of action is waiting, not knowing what next, and not having a glib answer."[4]

We might say that the process of actively pursuing or waiting on God ignites an inner work for the pray-er. There is this sense in the midst of the attitude and action of waiting that the prayer is not so much about the intervention desired but the activity of being with God. Hope is linked more to God's manifest presence than what we want him to do for us.

Being granted my petition is often good—healing for a friend, purpose for a family member, provision for the church—but of greater importance is the realization of the fullness of God's presence, affection, and faithfulness. In those moments of waiting, we realize that "*every good and perfect gift comes from the Father above*,"[5] and the best gift of all is HIMSELF.

---

3   Isaiah 64:4

4   Merton, *Conjectures of a Guilty Bystander*, p. 156

5   James 1:17.

Tarrying or waiting can produce the stillness of soul where we become alert to God's presence in our lives. But, I repeat, waiting is not passive.

In the tone of the Psalms that exhort us to wait on the Lord, we can feel a sense of urgency. The psalmist prays in the face of a challenging or difficult situation. The urgency or desperation is what motivates the prayer. The waiting is punctuated with courage, strength, trust, and help—all coming from the Lord.

Wait for the LORD; be strong, and let your heart take courage; wait for the LORD![6]

Be strong, and let your heart take courage, all you who wait for the LORD![7]

Our soul waits for the LORD; he is our help and our shield.[8]

I am weary with my crying out; my throat is parched. My eyes grow dim with waiting for my God.[9]

In the challenging situations, the praying psalmist is absolutely dependent on God's intervention and rescue. He is dead to self and any self-recovery. God is the only solution.

---

6   Psalm 27:14

7   Psalm 31:24

8   Psalm 33:20

9   Psalm 69:3

For God alone my soul waits in silence; from him comes my salvation.[10]

For God alone, O my soul, wait in silence, for my hope is from him.[11]

And now, O Lord, for what do I wait? My hope is in you.[12]

If we only view these passages as transactional prayers, then we see waiting as an act of endurance, waiting until the prayer gets what he or she wants. However, within the process of waiting there is something that moves the soul to a place of stillness and trust. The psalmist is waiting for the Lord.

But for you, O LORD, do I wait; it is you, O Lord my God, who will answer.[13]

I waited patiently for the LORD; he inclined to me and heard my cry.[14]

Again, in the process of praying, the psalmist experiences an inner comfort in realizing God's presence. Psalm 130 carries the

---

10   Psalm 62:1

11   Psalm 62:5

12   Psalm 39:7

13   Psalm 38:15

14   Psalm 40:1

title *My Soul Waits for the Lord.* Then twice in the psalm, the pray-er connects the process of waiting to the security of the soul or the inner person.

I wait for the LORD, my soul waits, and in his word I hope.[15]

My soul waits for the Lord more than watchmen for the morning, more than watchmen for the morning.[16]

There is a peace and inner joy that happen as a result of being connected to God in expectation. For the psalmist of Psalm 130, hope increased through a process of proactive and attentive waiting, as though his sense of the presence of God became more palpable through the waiting.

In his short devotional book, *Waiting on God*, Andrew Murray helped me understand waiting as an important aspect of prayer. The book was first published in 1896. I think of that time as so much simpler than the times in which we live. Yet when I read Murray's reflections on waiting, I see the same challenges in his day as we experience today. I imagine that Murray would have said that the times of the psalmists felt simpler than his own as well. Life has a way of taking over like aggressive weeds in a beautiful garden. We need to work at tending to the garden of our inner person. We do this by waiting on God.

Waiting on God is not easy to explain. It is a learned disposition in prayer. Maybe some of the following quotes from

---

15   Psalm 130:5

16   Psalm 130:6

Murray will add some nuance to our understanding.

[In] Prayer ... our waiting upon God must be exercised. ... it will indeed become the strength and the joy of the soul. Life will become one deep blessed cry: "I have waited by thy salvation, O Lord."[17]

The great aim would be to bring everyone in a praying and worshipping company under a deep sense of God's presence, so that when they part there will be the consciousness of having met God Himself, of having left every request with Him, and of now waiting in stillness while He works out His salvation. ... so conscious of his presence ... Waiting before God, and waiting for God, are the one condition of showing His presence. . . to wait on God alone ...[18]

The giver is more than the gift; God is more than the blessing; and our being kept waiting on Him is the only way for our learning to find our life and joy in *Himself*.[19]

What a dignity and blessedness to be attendants-in-waiting on the everlasting God, ever on the watch for every indication of His will or favor, ever conscious of His nearness, His

---

17   Murray, *Waiting on God*, p. 36

18   Murray, *Waiting on God*, p. 94–95

19   Murray, *Waiting on God*, p. 102

goodness, and His grace![20]

As long as waiting on God is chiefly regarded as an end toward more effectual prayer, the obtaining of our petitions, this spirit of perfect quietness will not be obtained. But when it is seen that the waiting on God is itself an unspeakable blessedness, one of the highest forms of fellowship with the Holy One, the adoration of Him in His glory will of necessity humble the soul into a holy stillness, making way for God to speak and reveal Himself.[21]

Attendants-in-waiting! That is trust. Waiting prayer enlarges that trust.

As I follow the thoughts of Murray, I see that the reward of waiting is far more than having my petition granted by God. In the process of waiting in prayer, God becomes larger. In the conversation, he becomes everything. We still want his intervention. We still want his salvation. But behind every longing is God himself. He is the hole in our heart that we are trying to fill. And if we will give ourselves to the process of waiting, he will become more precious to us than any secured answer to prayer.

Hudson Taylor also discovered this inner reward of waiting on God. His pursuit of God is chronicled in *Hudson Taylor's Spiritual Secret*. Taylor was a missionary to China in the late nineteenth century. Though fruitful in his labors, he noted how the labors depleted him. It was in waiting on God in prayer that

---

20   Murray, *Waiting on God*, p. 103

21   Murray, *Waiting on God*, p. 123–124

he discovered what he referred to as the exchanged life. As with the psalmists above, he realized that God alone was his salvation.

His circumstances did not necessarily change. The opposition to the gospel was not any less severe. But he became different through the abiding presence of Christ even in the midst of waiting. That presence was realized in tarrying prayer.

> Never again did the unsatisfied days come back; never again was the needy soul separated from the fullness of Christ. Trials came, deeper and more searching than ever before, but in them all joy flowed unhindered from the presence of the Lord Himself.[22]

Taylor would write in a letter, "I am no longer anxious about anything … for He is mine, and is with me and dwells in me."[23]

The exchanged life. Andrew Murray called it the Christ life. We die to our own efforts, and Christ is formed in us to accomplish his great transformative work.

Even the thought of waiting makes some of us anxious. Observe a person waiting for the delayed elevator. He keeps pushing the call button as if that would speed up the arrival of the elevator. Hudson Taylor found reward in the process of waiting itself, and the ultimate reward was God Himself.

The invitation to you is to rest in that same pool of Shalom. The Apostle Paul describes prayer as a peace-rendering activity.

---

22   Taylor, *Hudson Taylor's Spiritual Secret*, p. 117

23   Taylor, *Hudson Taylor's Spiritual Secret*, p. 117–118

The Lord is at hand; do not be anxious about anything, but in everything by prayer and supplication with thanksgiving let your requests be made known to God. And the peace of God, which surpasses all understanding, will guard your hearts and your minds in Christ Jesus.[24]

The Lord is at hand—near! Anxiety is not necessary. Prayer and supplication are a space of acknowledging our need for God's salvation. He makes the exchange with us: our anxiety for his all-consuming peace. Shalom.

My experience suggests that this type of understanding can occur on the corporate or community level. While pastoring in our church in Connecticut, I and the church family had to learn that principle of waiting. Over a three-year period, God brought a dynamic ministry team together. The process was a series of mysterious God movements. However, the initial hire took nearly two years. We had regularly scheduled corporate prayer times as we waited. The message God kept giving to me and to the search committee was "wait." I communicated this message from the pulpit and in writing multiple times over those two years. We waited, and then we waited some more. The result was that we received God's best rather than our perceived good—a good that was driven more by expediency or impatience than by excellence. God was putting this team together. It began with waiting on God and following his plan. I will tell more of how this plan unfolded in Chapter 29.

This is what Jesus did regularly. He waited in prayer.

---

24   Philippians 4:5b–7

Everything Jesus did was saturated in prayer. This is why he could say, "I only go where the Father is going, I only do what the Father is doing, and I only say what I hear the Father saying." This is the real essence of relational, dialogical, and two-way prayer.

In one of my staff meetings, I was leading a meditation on Advent waiting. We read and discussed the stories of Simeon and Anna who blessed the baby Jesus when his parents presented him at the Temple.[25] Both Simeon and Anna were older, godly people who had been waiting on the Lord for a long time. Their waiting was representative of a longer waiting of the people of God—hundreds of years.

Anna was eighty-four years old and by normal calculations she had been proactively waiting for the Messiah for about sixty years. Twice in the passage the word "waiting" is used. Part of the process of experiencing God's intervention is waiting; it always has been that way for his people. One member of our pastoral team captured it well: "Waiting is who we are." That is it. Waiting is not what we do; waiting is at the core of who we are as kingdom of God-expectant people who pray.

Your kingdom come, your will be done, on earth as it is in heaven. WAITING!

Active waiting is essential to the advancement of our spiritual life. Henri Nouwen notes, "Waiting as a disciple of Jesus is not empty waiting. It is waiting for the promise hidden in our hearts, which makes already present what we wait for."[26] In this sense, waiting is not about the future but about being

---

25   Luke 2:22–38.

26   Nouwen, *Discernment: Reading the Signs of Daily Life*, p. 150

fully present in the now as God unfolds his tomorrow for us. It is where real trust is formed, and trust is the bedrock of our relationship with the Lord.

At this stage of my life, I am seeing things come to fruition in magnificent ways, and some of these realizations are things I have been praying about for over thirty years. If only for having kept my hand in God's during this time, the result of waiting has been a gift.

Waiting prayer is a gift to challenge a modern problem, the fast pace of life. We are "instant" people. We are people on the move. We forget to slow down. As a result, we lack patience. And we lack peace. It is a spiritual problem.

Waiting is an act of faith.

Delayed gratification is a prerequisite to trust.

As people who pray for God's kingdom to come, we are not passive in the waiting. We wait with expectation. Paul captures it well in his letter to the Romans, *"But if we hope for what we do not see, we wait for it in patience."*[27] In this same chapter of Romans, Paul reminds us that we do not know what to pray for, so the Holy Spirit prays through us in groans and that he also intercedes on our behalf. Paul continues by noting that even creation (the cosmos, the earth) itself groans. Could the groaning of creation itself be a sort of intercession before God? All I know is that the wait provides the best gift of all: alertness to God's presence.

---

27   Romans 8:25

PRACTICAL EXERCISES

Make a list of God interventions that you have been waiting for. Then, for the next week, actively speak these requests out to the Lord—verbalize them.

Lord, I want to see....

And when you are done, thank him for the wait. Tell him that the wait has made you desperate for his intervention. Tell him that in the future wait, you will look through a lens focused on his presence more than his provision.

11

TOMMY

Everything that one turns in the direction of God is prayer.

—IGNATIUS OF LOYOLA[1]

MY LEVEL OF EXPECTANCY was off the charts. I had been in the community for just over two years. My prayer to God was for a demonstration of the gospel of the kingdom to bring a greater harvest. To give a sense of the context, I need to explain some of my core beliefs.

First, I do not believe that God rescues us so that we might first and foremost find a life of comfort or luxuriate in his presence. We have been promised eternal life for luxuriating and finding ultimate rest. Jesus said things like, "*Work for the night is coming,*"[2] or "*As the Father has sent me, I am sending you,*"[3] or

---

1   Hutchinson, *Six Ways to Pray from Six Great Saints*, p. 62

2   John 9:4

3   John 20:21

"Go make disciples of all nations."[4] The early disciples understood clearly that they had been rescued by God's grace, not their own efforts. However, this rescue was to reposition them as agents of witness to his grace. They gave of themselves, even unto martyrdom, to get that message out to as many people as possible. This belief can be expressed as the following principle:

Principle #1: We have been rescued in order to be agents in God's plan to rescue others and restore them to the kingdom.

Secondly, I believe that God does not gather people together as a local expression of his church to spend most of its (their) waking hours and budget dollars thinking about how to care for themselves. The local churches that Jesus addresses in the first few chapters of Revelation are called lampstands. A lampstand exists for one primary purpose: to extinguish the darkness. This purpose was the continuation of the work of Jesus: *"the light has come into the darkness and the darkness has not overcome it."*[5] The church is meaningless without a vibrant witness in its pagan community.

Principle #2: The church must be on mission. It exists primarily for its not-yet members.

Thirdly, God has called us to a style and application of ministry that the incarnate Jesus himself modeled. Clearly one aspect of his ministry is unrepeatable, crucifixion and resurrection in

---

4   Matthew 28:18–20

5   John 1:5

the literal sense. Instead, we are called to die to our selves and to live in him. Knowing that there are aspects of the work of Christ that we cannot replicate and knowing that we can do nothing without his life coursing through our veins, we are still called to operate in the Jesus way. So, we need to ask ourselves, *how did Jesus reach the masses?*

His method was threefold: announce the Good News of the kingdom, heal the sick, and cast out demons. Announcing is verbalizing. Healing and casting out are demonstrating. The Good News of the kingdom of God is validated in demonstration.

We do not have a faith that embraces word only but a faith of word and deed, proclamation and demonstration. When Jesus announced the beginning of his ministry at his hometown synagogue in Nazareth, he stated that the manifestation of the kingdom would be evident in *liberty to captives, recovering of sight to the blind, liberty to the oppressed, the Lord's favor.*[6] Everywhere that Jesus traveled, kingdom manifestation was the result; "*and he healed many who were sick with various diseases, and cast out many demons.*"[7]

Later in his ministry, John the Baptist sent a delegation to ask Jesus if he was indeed the Messiah, the Christ. Jesus answered by telling the delegation to report what they had heard and seen: "*The blind receive their sight and the lame walk, lepers are cleansed and the deaf hear, and the dead are raised up, and the poor have good news preached to them.*"[8] The affirmation of Christ

---

6   Luke 4:18–19

7   Mark 1:34

8   Matthew 11:5

and his teachings about the kingdom was in the demonstration of the kingdom.

The disciples followed the same pattern of ministry that Jesus did. When Jesus sent his disciples out, they announced the kingdom, healed the sick, and cast out demons.[9] Jesus, looking down the corridors of history, said that those who believed in him would do the things that he did and even greater.[10]

The early church was immersed in divine intervention, described as signs and wonders.[11] In fact, one of the main points of Acts of the Apostles is that the followers of Christ carried on the work of Jesus. The Jesus stuff did not stop with Jesus. We see this continuation of the works of Jesus in the experiences of Philip while he was on mission in Samaria to *"proclaim to them Christ."*[12] We are told that his message was heard not only because of the quality of the message but also because of the demonstration of the kingdom of God through *"the signs that he did."*[13] Throughout the accounts of the early church in Acts, we observe both miracles of restoration and judgment that affirmed the Word of God and accompanied its spreading influence.

The apostle Paul's missionary journeys were also laced with power. Paul, when writing to the church in Corinth, noted

---

9 Luke 9–10

10 John 14:12

11 Acts 2:43

12 Acts 8:4

13 Acts 8:5

that his speech and his message *"were not in plausible words of wisdom, but in demonstration of the Spirit and of power ... so that your faith might not rest on the wisdom of men but in the power of God."*[14] We know that he is not saying here that his message was unintelligible. His point was that the acceptance of the message did not hinge solely on its delivery, but also relied on the accompanying release of power for healing, deliverance, and divine intervention. The release of Holy Spirit power energizes the whole process. My point in giving all these biblical examples can be expressed in Principle #3:

Principle #3: The contemporary church should not expect to have success by acting in a different manner than Jesus and the early church.

With these three principles serving as the core of my beliefs, when I arrived at my new post for service in Connecticut, I prayed and waited in expectancy for God to demonstrate his kingdom. In the meantime, we took initiative in faith in asking him to intervene in the brokenness of lives around us. My prayer was not complicated:

Jesus, if your ministry was validated by demonstration, if the early church's ministry was validated by demonstration, if the apostle Paul's ministry was validated by demonstration, how are we to penetrate our society that is post-Christian and secularized, and over-comfortable, if you do not release demonstration?

---

14   I Corinthians 2:4–5

So, I prayed with expectancy, and I led others to prayer with expectancy.

Then the opportunity came!

"Our pastor is here, and I have asked him to pray for Tommy." I was sure that this was the moment that we had been waiting and praying for. God had orchestrated an opportunity to point to the glory of Jesus and thus advance the gospel message in our community.

A new family had come to our church. They had been introduced to our church, and the wife especially was intrigued by the vibrancy of faith evident in our church family and gatherings. Tommy,[15] her brother in-law, had been diagnosed with an aggressive form of cancer. He was a young father, and they were pursuing every type of new medical discovery to combat the disease. He was about travel to another country for a new procedure. This family was well-connected in the larger community, and so there was shared concern in the larger community. That evening, a large number of influential people were gathered in their home to send Tommy off with well wishes. My wife and I responded to the invitation to do the same.

"Our pastor is here." I was moved by that simple phrase. They had only attended our church for a short time, yet I was given a place in the family.

"I have asked him to pray for Tommy." Faith—publicly declared faith—that is the response that Jesus delighted in when he walked on the earth.

What an opportunity! I wanted the healing for Tommy's

---

15   Name changed in respect for the family who experienced loss.

sake. Who doesn't feel compassion when a young father is fighting a life-threatening disease?

I wanted the healing for the host family's sake. They were at the beginning of understanding and entry into a faith journey with Jesus. I wanted the healing for the wife. I wanted it for the husband. I wanted it for their children. I wanted it for their extended family. I wanted the healing for the sake of every influential person gathered in that home. This would be the open door to trusting the crucified and resurrected Christ, and a fresh revelation that he is the same yesterday, today, and forever.[16]

I wanted the healing ultimately for the glory of Jesus. He is most glorified when his distant children are reconciled to him. "Faith comes through hearing, and hearing through the word of Christ."[17] And as I noted earlier, the word of Christ is affirmed through the demonstration of Christ.

So, I moved to the middle of the living room, and I prayed a simple and bold prayer. I gave thanks to God for the medical profession and advancements that we see in our days. I gave glory to Jesus as the bearer of our sins and ultimate healer. I prayed with authority against the disease, and I prayed with expectancy for a release of God's bounty in the body of Tommy. Amen!

Now it was time for God to do his part.

I live and lead passionately out of the Word of God, but one scripture especially drives me and gives shape to how I view my presence in this world.

---

16   Hebrews 13:8

17   Romans 10:17

The Lord is not slow to fulfill his promise as some count slowness, but is patient toward you, not wishing that any should perish, but that all should reach repentance.[18]

As one who has been liberated through God's patience, I want the same for everyone in my community. I view my life as a partnership with him toward the same end. I am always expecting movements of God. So, whenever possible, I have prayed openly for healing and deliverance with people in our area, and I do not restrict this to the people in the church. There are moments that are clearly orchestrated situations to point to the glory and love of my God who does not want any to perish. Surrounded by Tommy's family, I believed I was standing in the midst of such a moment.

This story does not have a good ending, at least from my current vantage point. Tommy's physical health deteriorated, and he died. In the years following, the family experienced more trouble, including internal strife and broken relationships. Though I was honored to continue to be their pastor by conducting Tommy's memorial service, I did not experience what I wanted in prayer: healing for a longer and abundant life for Tommy on this earth and ultimate healing in a release of eternal life for all those looking on.

I was disappointed. It seemed like the perfect time for God to work. Even though I know that his ways are not my ways, I was still disappointed. I cannot understand everything, and I certainly do not see the life circumstances around me from his vantage

---

18   II Peter 3:9

point. I also know that it is foolish to interpret the story in the middle. There may be a chapter ahead that mysteriously flows out of what I perceive as a missed opportunity by God to point to his active presence in our world. Nevertheless, I cannot help but view the situation from what I do see and what I do know.

God is healer. That day, he decided not to heal—at least physically.

God is demonstrator of his kingdom. That day, he decided not to miraculously demonstrate his kingdom.

So, the challenge of prayer is when it feels like God has not responded. I address the issue of disappointment in the next chapter.

PRACTICAL EXERCISES

Make a list of the times when you have been disappointed in prayer. Try to feel the pain of that disappointment in a fresh way. Maybe you are in the middle of it, so the pain is already there.

Now give the pain to God in a prayer. Tell him how you feel.

Wait and listen. What is his response?

Write it down.

12

MYSTERY AND DISAPPOINTMENT

*It is hard, when difficulties arise to know whether one is meant to over-
come them or whether they are signs that one is on the wrong track. I
suppose the deeper one's own life of prayer and sacraments the more
trustworthy one's judgment will be.*

−C.S. LEWIS[1]

*To clasp the hands in prayer is the beginning of an uprising against the
disorder of the world.*

−KARL BARTH[2]

THROUGHOUT THIS BOOK I am offering several accounts of what
I believe to be irrevocable testimony, if not **evidence,** pointing
to the reality of answered prayer. I concede that prayer is not
scientifically provable. I concede that I recount these situations

---

1   Lewis, *Yours, Jack,* p. 220

2   Barth, *Prayer,* p. 15

from my own, subjective point of view. All the same, some of these accounts are too eerie to simply write off as coincidence.

In offering these examples, I do not want to imply that every one of my prayers has been a straightforward success, as we often deem success in prayer. I have been disappointed in the results of my prayer many times, as the story of Tommy in the previous chapter demonstrates. There have been many moments in my life when at the time I was sure that my prayer request aligned well with what I know of God. He is a merciful God. He does answer the prayer of those who wait on him. He celebrates faith that asks boldly. He desires for all people to be restored to vibrant relationship with him. I was surprised when God did not respond **as I desired**—and by the way, my desires in many of those situations offered no personal gain to me.

Many of us do not question the reality of prayer because we have had circumstances or situations that are hard to explain otherwise—a healing, an unexplainable provision or guidance, a suspension of natural order. The real challenge comes in the times when prayer seems to go unanswered—or not answered in a way that we would expect a good God to respond—or harder yet, when the response seems to be "no."

Sometimes, it can feel that prayer testimonies feel rather arbitrary. An example is God healing my ankle at the prayer service but not (yet) healing my friend who remains paralyzed in a wheelchair for whom I have been praying for over ten years. Or the time that God miraculously answered my prayer for provision in providing scholarships for my kids for university, in light of the other times when he did not respond affirmatively when I asked him to intervene for friends who were experiencing more severe financial disaster. Thus, the correlation of prayer to results, and what might be called the urgency of need, continually remains a mystery to us, but this is no reason not to pray.

If I were to have kept a scoresheet through my life of prayers answered the way I wanted versus prayers that were not answered the way I wanted, I would probably be losing. Now, it is a good thing that many of my prayers were not answered the way I wanted. I heard Ruth Graham Lotz quote her mother Ruth Bell Graham as saying, "God has not always answered my prayers. If He had, I would have married the wrong man—several times!"[3] We understand that sometimes God's "no" to certain prayers is a gift. However, it is much harder when the "no" feels so senseless or distant from what we would expect from a loving and powerful God.

One of my favorite books on prayer is entitled *Prayer* by Philip Yancey. The reason I like Yancey as an author and why I read him so much is because we seem to have extreme opposite personality types. I have been blessed with a gift of faith: the cup is not just half full for me; it is often overflowing. I'm always looking for potential opportunities for the kingdom of God to break in to my own life and for others. I regularly take the risk of praying for people on the spot and in public. As I read Yancey, he seems to be more reserved and skeptical. He challenges weak presuppositions of Christians in his writing. He asks hard questions. He refuses simplistic answers. I need him to balance my life; I need his perspective. Understanding that perspective helps me in inviting others into faith initiatives.

---

3   Quote can be found in "Billy & Ruth Graham: Couple of Purity" on *Marked Ministry*, https://markedministry.com

In *Prayer*, Yancey asks the hard questions of prayer that easily get glossed over in faith traditions. He is not reluctant to recount the times he prayed and God responded as Yancey desired, but he is also honest about all the times he prayed or someone else prayed and it seemed that God did nothing. It is this mystery of prayer that keeps him grounded, avoiding any type of presumption or to reduce prayer to a formula—the idea that God owes me my predetermined response when I pray with faith. Yancey quotes a philosophy professor to illustrate the complexity surrounding the mystery of prayer, "If God can influence the course of events, then the God who is willing to cure colds or provide parking spaces but who is not willing to prevent Auschwitz or Hiroshima is morally repugnant."[4] We are left with the lingering mysteries and questions surrounding the apparent randomness to God's response to our prayer.

So, with this complexity of experience and testimony, how are we to hold on to prayer in an honest and yet faith-filled manner? Some people have simply dismissed prayer because of the complexity or mystery. This dismissal can be wrapped into theologies that minimalize prayer or minimalize the impact of prayer by suggesting that we should neither ask specifically nor boldly. The problem is that Scripture puts a high value on faith-filled prayer; therefore, we cannot simply dismiss it.

Scripture exhorts us to pray. The Psalms are the praise and prayers of the people of God who have gone before us. Jesus invites his followers into a practice of prayer. Throughout the Bible, prayer is recommended and commanded with lots of promises.

---

4   Yancey, *Prayer*, p. 74

I have chosen to embrace the full mystery of prayer. If I am honest, the mystery hasn't driven me away from prayer, but enhances my prayer life. Now, this may be related to how I am designed: I am comfortable with dissonance, I like change, I do fine not knowing a plan or outcome, and I have little need for control. Where embracing mystery might be easy for me, I realize that it might be more challenging for others.

I feel the mystery also keeps me honest before God. We are in relationship. It is easy to manipulate in relationship. It would be easy to have an expectation that God is my personal genie, but it is dangerous to put Almighty God in my obligatory bottle.

Along my own pilgrimage, I had neater explanations of prayer when I was younger in the faith. Today, I have fewer black-and-white answers, but I believe that my prayer life is richer and fuller today in the middle of mystery. As a result, my prayers are less transactional and more relational. God and I, and God and we (my praying community), are in conversation, which is built on principles of relationship far more than rules.

Some people have pointed out to me the negative potential of praying if God does not respond according to our request. It can be a bit disillusioning to get "no" for a response. But is disillusionment a bad thing? I do not want to establish my life on illusion. Weak philosophies and theologies may feel good for the moment, but they will not support messy life. We need illusions removed from our prayer life, our primary place of dialogue and partnership with God.

For example, if we reduce our understanding of prayer to a formula of "ask and get," we will be disappointed. If we treat God as the Great Keeper of the Heavenly Candy Store, and our currency to get what we want from that store is prayer, we will be disappointed.

Prayer is far more complex and mysterious because any relationship is that way.

Furthermore, responding to those with questions with quick and ready maxims and adages about prayer may capture certain aspects of the theology of prayer, but these facile, oversimplified responses will always leave some people lurching in their faith. If we explore the Bible honestly, we will see that, more than hard and fast rules, the Word of God gives us principles about prayer. Rules make us rigid. Principles allow us to embrace the grey areas of mystery. Next, I want to look at two notions that I have heard about prayer and that I find detrimental to faith and the life of prayer.

GOD ALWAYS ANSWERS PRAYER: YES, NO, NOT YET!

When a person has been frustrated after a long period of continual intercession, she may declare, "Maybe God answers your prayer, but he does not answer mine." The quick and ready response might be "God always answers prayer: yes, no, or not yet!"

Now, there is a kernel of truth embedded in this response. However, it can feel a bit harsh to the person who waits in the silence and tries to guess which of the two final possibilities God intends, no or not yet? If God's answer is "no," then the pray-er can resolve to accept, trust, and move on. If it is "not yet," then the pray-er can ask for courage, trust, and pray on. If only God made it clearer!

Jesus taught in the parable of the Persistent Widow[5] that

---

5   Luke 18

perseverance is rewarded in prayer. The challenge is in the waiting and wondering. Easy answers about prayer may trivialize how mysterious the dialogue of prayer really is. Worse yet, it may trivialize the feelings of the person desperately wrestling in prayer.

Hear the cries of the psalmists in the Imprecatory Psalms. *How long, O God? Hear my prayer! Why do you remain silent?* These are all expressions of frustration in prayer. God is neither embarrassed nor perturbed by these cries as evidenced by the fact that he has chosen to guard them in Holy Writ. Eventually the psalmist declares his trust in God, even in the mystery of the silence. However, it was the process of prayer that was important. Likewise, we need to give others the freedom to wrestle in the midst of the mystery.

Maybe the better response to the person who feels that God is not responding would be, "It sounds like you are frustrated in the long wait. I can understand that frustration, as I have been disappointed in prayer at times. And the psalmists and prophets were often frustrated with the silences and delays of God. I hope you get fresh courage to keep on praying." Maybe even better yet would be to offer to join the person in the arduous pursuit of God for an intervention.

Thus, I find the response "yes, no, not yet" containing truth but missing the components of care and reality.

IF ONLY YOU HAD MORE FAITH

I know a number of people who have come to the conclusion (or had it suggested to them) that the reason their prayer was not answered with "yes" and "right away" was because they lacked faith. Now, it is true that some prayers are ineffective because of a lack of faith. Mark writes in his gospel that when Jesus returned to his hometown, he could only do a few miracles there because of their unbelief.[6] It sounds like some kingdom breakthroughs were blocked because of a lack of faith.

Jesus regularly commended faith as a doorway to kingdom release. He marvels at two things: great faith and lack of faith. However, faith is a *principle* for the practice of effectual prayer, not a *rule* that guarantees certain results in prayer. I can explain this from both Scripture and from personal experience.

Hebrews 11 is referred to as the great chapter of faith. The chapter opens with this strong declaration: "without faith it is impossible to please God. . . and that he rewards those who seek him."[7] After this declaration, one person of faith after another is recounted as victorious because of their faith. Through faith they conquered kingdoms, enforced justice, obtained promises, stopped the mouths of lions, quenched the power of fire, escaped the edge of the sword, were made strong out of weakness, became mighty in war, and put foreign armies to flight.[8] Those sound like big "YES" responses to the faith of people who would have been asking and trusting God for clear interventions in the face of opposition and trouble.

If the chapter ended here, it would support a rigid or mechanical connection between faith and results in prayer. However, the chapter does not end here; this list of positive outcomes of faith is followed by another list of faith-filled people who

---

6   Mark 6

7   Hebrews 11:6

8   Hebrews 11:33–34

experienced different results. Some received back their family, dead; some were tortured; some suffered mocking, flogging, chains of imprisonment; others were stoned, sawn in two, or killed with the sword.[9] My guess is that in most of those cases these faith-filled people were praying for something else, and at least one or two of the people cried out to God with faith. If not, why would they be included in the chapter of faith? In some faith-healing contexts, they would be rebuked for their lack of faith and even blamed for what they did not receive.

For me, given these two sets of outcomes to great faith, I cannot reduce "unanswered" prayer or "unrealized" desires in prayer to the sole issue of faith. A lack of faith may block results, but we should not automatically be concluding this about people who have had enough faith to pray or ask for prayer. The initiative to pray or seek prayer seems to be enough faith—a mustard seed-sized faith. My own life experience confirms this reality, both positively and negatively.

We have some interesting prayer testimonies from when my family lived in France for language study. When we arrived, I began an early morning prayer gathering with fellow students who were learning French to be missionaries in different corners of the world—France, Belgium, Haiti, and parts of Africa. Our group experienced direct answers to prayer over the course of the year. Later, several of the missionaries began an English service on Sunday evenings and experienced another wave of divine interventions to prayer. Ingrid, my wife, experienced severe back pain. During one of those services her back was dramatically

---

9   Hebrews 11:35–37

healed. God responded to Ingrid's faith in requesting prayer and to the faith of the group in praying. It was a dramatic physical manifestation and change.

Some months after Ingrid's healing, I was experiencing back trouble. It reached the point where I could not sit in class. I, too, asked for prayer. However, I did not experience the same immediate intervention that Ingrid received. In order to continue with my studies, I would stand in the back of the classroom during lessons, but eventually even standing was too painful. So, finally, one day, I left class early and returned to our apartment frustrated.

I lay down on the floor in our little apartment. To be quite honest, I was not praying but grumbling. This was a "cup half empty" day for me. A friend had loaned us a videotape weeks earlier that had been sent to her by family. It was a sermon from a well-known pastor from Texas. I felt led to put the tape into the VCR. The preacher began expounding on the topic of healing. As he preached, a warm sensation hit my back. I knew God was touching me.

Anointing through a VHS tape?

I only discovered later that he was well known in Texas and had a healing ministry. This fact was unknown to me prior to watching the video.

The reason that this story is so important to me is that I was healed without an expression of believing faith, on my part, at that moment. Since this experience, in all of the moments where I have experienced God's intervention in prayer, for me or through me, it has diminished the value that I have put in my own faith. The operative force in prayer is not my faith but God and the finished work of Christ. This helps me keep *faith* as an underlying principle, rather than a rule, in the context of prayer.

Finally, **how much faith is enough?** Is there a tipping point? Jesus said, "If you have the faith the size of a mustard seed, you could cast a mountain into the sea."[10] His point is quite clear: a little bit goes a long way. It is not that you must amass enough faith to create the tipping point. The faith to have the initial thought and to ask for intervention seems to be enough.

There are other destructive maxims and explanations for prayer. In this chapter, I have chosen these two because I hear them most frequently. The first, though correct, is demotivating through its lack of compassion for the person in the middle of the prayer struggle. The second, though sometimes correct, is accusatory, as it does not speak to all situations and leans more toward prayer rules than prayer principles.

I have chosen to eliminate easy formulas from my theology of prayer and embrace fully the mystery of prayer. Mystery has not demotivated me at all from praying as some faith movements would suggest. Instead, it has strengthened the honesty of my relationship with God and the kindness of my relationship with others. In the end, I cannot fully explain prayer. I have been gloriously surprised by its results. I have been glaringly disappointed by its failures—or at least failure as I interpret it. With fewer answers today, I embrace the mystery, and I choose to pray more than ever.

---

10   Matthew 17:20

When have you been significantly disappointed by a "no" response in prayer? How have you processed that disappointment?

In thinking about that disappointment, where have your notions of God and your relationship with him been askew?

Are you willing to pray the following prayer?

> *Lord, I want a real relationship with you. I want our prayer conversation to be well beyond a transactional formula. I am willing to embrace the mystery of prayer—not completely understanding it but still pressing fully into it. I will tell you when I am confused or disappointed. I will trust through the challenge of that dialogue. In Jesus, Amen.*

13

DENISE

The praying life is the abiding life.

—PAUL E. MILLER[1]

PRAYER FLOWS OUT OF RELATIONSHIP. Relationship is fluid and not static. Mere distance can make us feel disconnected from family and friends. Similarly, we may have life experiences that cause us to draw away from God.

Generally, we tend to think only of sin as a cause of rupture in the relationship. However, unmet expectations can also create relational distance. When we experience difficult life circumstances, we can feel that God has been silent in the midst of our pain. Tragedy can push us over the edge.

I have good friends by the names of Radwan and Denise Dagher. Radwan was a student at the seminary where I taught. He was more like my brother than a student. We had both

---

1   Miller, *A Praying Life*, p. 122

been missionaries in West Africa during the same time period. He was from Lebanon, and I was from the United States, but our life stories were very similar. We even had similar persons of influence in our lives even though we grew up on different continents. He was at the seminary to gain training to return to Lebanon as director of the Bible School.

After his studies, Radwan returned with his family to lead the Bible School. Within a short time, he contracted viral meningitis and tragically died. It was one of the saddest pieces of personal news that I had ever received. The Middle East needs well-trained Christian leaders. God does not have a problem when we ask questions in prayer. The Psalms are full of hard questions in prayer. And I had some hard questions about this situation.

Why send the Daghers to America for study and then allow him to die so suddenly before fully entering into his assignment?

This was confusing for me. God, what are you doing? In my relational conversation with the Father, I've come to embrace the understanding that he owes me no explanation, but he doesn't mind me asking. Isn't this what relationship is about: shared joy and shared disappointment?

My wife and I saw Denise about a year later and asked her how she was processing the grief of her loss. It was understandably hard for her. Her strength came through praying **in community**. She was at a point where she was having a hard time praying, so her friends established the "Denise Dagher Prayer Support Group." They prayed for her—carried her to Jesus—like the four friends in the gospel who carry the lame man to Jesus on a mat. In time, she was able to voice herself to the Lord, but it was still a process. I will never forget what she said that day we met, a year after Radwan's death: "I'm not able to look God in the face yet, but I've gotten to the point that I can crawl up into his lap."

What beautiful words. Even in a life of disappointed expectations, God the Father is still breathing comfort and presence over us by his Spirit. We just need to keep showing up. Waiting, crawling, standing, walking, running, mounting with wings as eagles. In time, we will again be able to hear him whisper that our standing as sons and daughters is still safe even though the world we live in is not always safe.

The Apostle Paul reminds us that by His Spirit, God declares "Abba! Father" into our hearts.[2] We especially need that in times of disappointment when it feels like God has turned his gaze away. Our groan mingled with his groan might be the best prayer that we can offer at a moment of disappointment.

---

2   Galatians 4:6

PART II

JESUS AND PRAYER

THE WORDS ARE BOTH INSPIRING AND HAUNTING to me. "I don't think we're going to get out of this thing; I'm going to have to go out on faith." Then, together with the operator on the other end of the phone line they prayed, "Our Father who art in heaven, hallowed be Thy name ..."

Some of you will recognize these as the words of Todd Beamer, who was on the hijacked flight United 93 on September 11, 2001, that crashed into the Pennsylvania countryside. It is believed this plane, in the hands of hijackers, was headed toward either the Capitol Building or the White House in Washington, D.C. In a moment of courage, passengers worked to overtake the hijackers before the plane crashed into the ground, giving themselves up so that something of national treasure and international influence would not be lost. They gave themselves to save the lives of others on the ground who would have been victims in the act of terror.

Todd prayed the Lord's Prayer with a woman named Lisa. She was the GE customer representative. It is said that Todd kept the Lord's Prayer as a bookmark when he was travelling. But Todd knew the prayer well because he was a fully engaged disciple of Jesus Christ. In his moment of crisis, when he would have to do something courageous, he went to that which was familiar to his heart, the Lord's Prayer. The prayer rallied his strength.

The next thing Lisa heard over the open phone line was Todd leading the other passengers in Psalm 23, another go-to Scripture for people in the face of death, which was followed by the words that are now associated for eternity with Todd Beamer: "Are you guys ready.... Let's roll."

The Lord's Prayer and Psalm 23. Words to live by and words to die by. Familiarity can cause us to flippantly or mindlessly recite these passages if we do not slow down or tune our hearts to the deep meanings behind the rhythms of recitation of these familiar passages. At the same time, the ritual of recitation can cement them deeply into our soul for those moments when extemporaneous prayer eludes us.

The Lord's Prayer can land anywhere on the spectrum for us, from deeply meaningful to meaningless ritual. The problem is not with the prayer but with our hearts and our circumstances. I want to call us to see the Lord's Prayer as a manifesto of hope and faith and as a model that can give direction to our more spontaneous prayer expression.

One of the keys to reinvest the prayer with meaning is to dive deeply into each phrase in the context of Jesus's world. In going deep into the context of this familiar prayer, we will never again be able to pray it casually. We discover that it unfolds five foundational blocks of prayer: praise, intercession, supplication, confession, and warfare. We also discover several attitudes embedded in the Lord's prayer that become essential to praying with confidence: submission, faith, trust, and ambassadorship.

Part II will begin with a discussion of Jesus as a pray-er. Philip Yancey states that the most compelling reason or motivation for praying is found in the simple fact that Jesus made prayer a priority in his own life. The implications embedded in his own practice is that **Jesus' example and invitation call every Christ-follower to develop a life of prayer**. His model prayer flows naturally from his own life of prayer. In the following sections, we will set the prayer into context of the first-century practice of Jewish prayer. However, an understanding of prayer without a practice of prayer is like a car manual without the car. Thus, several models of the Lord's Prayer will be given as practical tools to enrich and grow in your own practice of prayer.

Jesus commended the builder of a house who built on the rock and not the sand because such a house would stand in the storms of life. His interpretation of building on a rock was to be people who hear the Word and put it into practice—do it! As your understanding of prayer grows from the text, engage in the practice of prayer, even if it is the simple start of praying the daily prayers offered at the end of each chapter. As you enlarge your practice, you will find your life-house being built on the rock!

14

JESUS PRAYED AND
PRAYED AND PRAYED

The life we want in Christ is ours free, a gift of grace. And yet, experiencing that life on this side of eternity is a struggle.

—MIKE COSPER[1]

By praying the Psalms, we "pray along with Christ's prayer and therefore may be certain and glad that God hears us. When our will, our whole heart, enters into the prayer of Christ, then we are truly praying. We can pray only in Jesus Christ, with whom we shall all be heard."

DIETRICH BONHOEFFER[2]

LORD, TEACH US TO PRAY! As I said earlier, I find this to be an astonishing request from the early disciples who walked

---

1 Cosper, *Recapturing the Wonder*, p. 162

2 Metaxas, *Bonhoeffer: Pastor, Martyr, Prophet, Spy*

with Jesus, considering the many things that they could have requested. It appears that they made a connection between the proclamation and demonstration of the kingdom of God through Jesus and his prayer life.

It also must have been quite the experience to hear Jesus pray out of the intimacy of his relationship with the Father. I have had that experience of being in a room when someone so familiar and deeply connected with God prayed; it was like God actually walked into the room. When Jesus prayed, it was God-incarnate and God-in-heaven in the same throne room. That would be a vibrant dialogue to take in.

The biblical writers capture the intensity of Jesus' prayer. The writer of Hebrews notes that, "Jesus offered up prayers and supplications, with loud cries and tears ... and he was heard."[3] Based on the context of the passage, this description seems to refer to his anguished prayer in Gethsemane shortly before going to the cross. Mark tells us that this prayer came out of a deep sense of distress and that Jesus himself said, "My soul is very sorrowful, even unto death."[4] Luke describes the intensity of his earnest prayer as "his sweat became like great drops of blood falling down on the ground."[5] Jesus had an active prayer life.

Prayer is interlaced into every aspect of Jesus' life. There are nineteen references to Jesus praying in the Gospels, but we only have eight of his actual prayers. His longest is the Great High Priestly Prayer in John 17 where he prays for you and I

---

3   Hebrews 5:7

4   Mark 14:34

5   Luke 22:44

as a foreshadowing of his ongoing intercessory role in heaven to this day. His shortest prayer is, "Father, glorify your name."[6] Notably, that short prayer was met with an audible voice from heaven.

Jesus fulfilled his incarnational purpose in an ongoing conversation with the Father.

So, our first example to a life of prayer must begin with Jesus. We need to dive into the depth of his practice of prayer. How he prayed tells us more about prayer than the instructions that he left on prayer. And his continual role of intercession at the right hand of the Father, along with the Holy Spirit, speaks boldly about the ongoing value of prayer.

PRAYER AS PRIORITY FOR JESUS

Mark's Gospel begins with the adult life of Jesus. He does not record the birth narratives as Matthew and Luke do, and his historical recounting is packed with action. Nor does Mark record lengthy sections on Jesus's teaching like Matthew. Instead, Mark prefers to embed the teaching in the flow of the action. When reading Mark's gospel in one sitting, you are left breathing hard as you try to keep pace with Jesus and the disciples. This energetic pace is not surprising considering that Mark was believed to be a scribe for Peter, and Peter was the epitome of action.

In the first chapter alone of Mark's Gospel, the word *immediately* occurs twelve times. Mark likes action. His gospel is fast-paced. Mark does not waste any time in describing the bold manifestations of the kingdom:

---

6   John 12:28

- Jesus was inaugurated into ministry through baptism and Holy Spirit descent;

- He moved out into the wilderness for temptation and warfare with Satan;

- He began recruiting his disciples;

- He taught, healed, and cast out demons; and

- He did much of this with the masses.

Activity radiates from the words of that first chapter, but then, all of a sudden, we come to verse 35:

And rising very early in the morning, while it was still dark, he departed and went out to a desolate place, and there he prayed.

After all the activity, finding Jesus stopped in a quiet place and waiting is like coming to a screeching halt. The disciple who finds him wants to get back to the action, and we sense that he feels Jesus is wasting his time. However, Mark 1:35 is a declaration of the value Jesus put on prayer in the midst of an active ministry life.

"Jesus, early in the morning, while it was still dark." **Priority!**
Jesus lived the first fruits principle[7] even in his use of time.
Conversation with the Father was the key to a successful day.
Thus, before beginning anything else in his day, Jesus sought
to find space alone with the Father

Principle #1: If we don't make prayer a priority, then it will
always remain an add-on or second thought to navigating our day.

Prayer will not happen naturally in our lives. Only after
learning the discipline of prayer can it become an unconscious
attitude or action. Prayer can become our go-to response, but
that ability to flow in prayer in the course of life begins with
learning the discipline through prioritization.

"He departed and went out to a desolate place." This line
indicates **strategy**. Even Jesus needed quiet to pray. We can
pray anywhere, anytime, but if we don't settle into quiet places,
we will not be able to tune our ears to the Father's voice above
the noise of daily life.

Principle #2: Solitude is essential to tune and develop our
prayer ear.

Luke says that Jesus often went to solitary places to pray.[8]
The disciples seemed to wander upon him more than once

---

7   The first fruits principle is that we are more fruitful in life when we give back to
     God the best rather than waiting and giving him what is leftover. The principle is
     linked to the practice of tithing (giving 10% of produce or income to God) that was
     first applied in an agricultural or pastoral society and which many of us apply to our
     finances today. The foundation of the first fruits principle is that it all belongs to God
     anyhow—our time, our gifts and talents, our treasure—and we are just stewards or
     managers. Acknowledging God's bounty in our lives frees us up to use these resources
     but not become consumed by them.

8   Luke 4:42

"praying alone."[9] The very Son of God knew that everything that would happen through him would be the result of prayer, and prayer was learned in the practice and discipline of being apart from the noise of the world.

When reading the account of Jesus praying alone in Mark 1, one senses that the disciples were a bit frantic or frustrated with Jesus when they found him praying. "Everyone is looking for you."[10] The disciples wanted him to **do** more kingdom stuff. They wanted action. Yet Jesus was praying. Remember the phrase that you heard as a kid, "Don't just stand there, do something?" Jesus operated in a different order: "Don't just do something, stand there (in prayer)." Better yet, kneel there and pray. This is the antithesis to motion: waiting on God.

This pausing in prayer is not to suggest that Jesus was reluctant to act. Mark 1 is full of action. Jesus simply knew that prayer was an important step toward unleashing fruitful action. Prayer is not preparation for ministry (action); it is the beginning, or first action, of ministry.

Consider the importance of prayer to Jesus by these following accounts:

- He was baptized in water and with the Holy Spirit, but he didn't go out immediately and start preaching. Instead, he went immediately to the desert to fast, led by the Holy Spirit. In the biblical context, fasting means prayer.[11]

---

9   Luke 9:18

10   Mark 1:37

11   Matthew 4:1–11

- When Jesus called his disciples, Luke tells us that he first spent the night in prayer, and then chose his disciples. He was listening for guidance from the Father.[12]

- Before he raised Lazarus from the dead, Jesus prayed. His praying appears to have nothing to do with the resurrection; he raised Lazarus from the dead at the command of his voice, a declaration, not intercession. But his prayer was expressed to help the faith of those looking on.[13]

- When the disciples couldn't cast a demon out of a young boy, the father questions Jesus about their inability. Jesus declared, "These only come out by prayer."[14] His words are surprising because in the moments that follow, he casts the demon out by command and does not pray. In his comment, he was referring to the quality and necessity of his prayer life prior to the encounter.

- When Jesus was struggling in the Garden at Gethsemane before the cross, he found the strength to complete his mission through prayer.[15]

---

12   Luke 6:12–16

13   John 11:38–44

14   Mark 9:29

15   Luke 22:44

- The first and last words of Jesus on the cross were prayers: "Father, forgive them, . . ."[16] and "Father, into your hands I commit my spirit."[17] He prayed out of the pattern of his model prayer.

Jesus' example obviously marked the disciples because when they get a chance to request teaching they went right to the key: "Teach us how to pray." I've always found that interesting. I would expect the disciples to ask Jesus to teach them how to heal the sick, cast out demons, multiply bread, or even love well. Instead, they asked Jesus to teach them how to pray because they recognized that everything flowed from his relationship with the Father through prayer.

Prayer is where we partner with God. Without prayer, we will not experience our fully redeemed identity through Christ. We will never get to the point of having the kingdom impact that God designed for our lives. We will not explore the fullness of his relationship with us. Prayer is where it all begins and where it is maintained. I cannot have an ongoing relationship with God without prayer.

Karl Barth noted that it's impossible to know God without prayer. A theologian of his status could have discussed multiple deep ideas on the topic of pursuing God. However, in his heart, Barth knew that prayer was the most theologically profound thing that a person could do in order to know God intimately and experientially.

---

16   Luke 23:34

17   Luke 23:46

Prayer is also where the kingdom of God touches down in our world. It is in prayer that we tap into the full power of God. We are not able to produce anything for the kingdom of God; Jesus told us that we could do nothing without him, but everything through him.[18] He then linked this action to abiding; he is the vine and we are the branches. Abiding is another way of speaking of waiting or tarrying. It is proactively and intentionally remaining attached to the source.

What we do is create space for God to enter. That happens at the moment of prayer. It's those moments that we become a conduit between him and everything that he has done and wants to do for this world. God will come and change reality as we pray. We never know exactly what he will do or transform, so we must pray in every situation and at every turn, inviting him into those spaces. Maybe a better way to say it might be that, in prayer, we come to identify the places where his manifest presence is waiting to be revealed. God is already there. We are simply creating the space in our hearts for him to quicken our spiritual eyes to see and receive.

I love to look back and see the spaces where God has changed the atmosphere or the situation as we have partnered with him in prayer. The transformation hasn't been everything that I desired or envisioned. But having prayed, I can trust that I have always gotten what is best from his perspective. The transformation that I have witnessed is alone worth the waiting.

If we look at the history of the revival of the church, just about every time there was a movement of God, there was a

---

18   The Parable of the Vine and Branches in John 15

group of people who got so connected with God that they became lightning rods for what God wanted to do.

If we're honest, prayer is not easy for us. This difficulty should not surprise us as the Apostle Paul described prayer as struggle or wrestling.[19] Jacob wrestled with God. Moses needed help holding his arms and hands up in prayer. Jesus prayed in such anguish in Gethsemane that "his sweat became like great drops of blood falling to the ground."[20] Does anybody find prayer easy?

There are some people who have the gift of intercession, so it seems more natural for them. Prayer just seems to flow from them, and they find no tedium in spending long hours in conversation with God. However, even intercessors have to develop the gift that God has deposited within them. Prayer is discipline, and discipline is work. My mentor, Carl Tonnessen, learned to pray by spending time with God. He was a simple man who had been in Jesus's school of prayer through long practice, a simplicity that made him quite profound.

Though we can grow in the discipline of praying as with any discipline, there is a spiritual component to prayer that makes it always a struggle. Jesus exhorted his disciples to pray with this warning: "The spirit is willing, but the flesh is weak."[21] I get distracted, my mind moves into different places. I have to be very intentional about prayer. My flesh is given to comfort and laziness, not pressing in to know God and to engage Him in prayer. And

---

19   Colossians 4:12

20   Luke 22:44

21   Matthew 26:41

beyond that, I am not always sure what I should pray.

The Apostle Paul writes, "We don't know how to pray as we ought."[22] Paul is not talking about the mechanics of prayer. He is talking about the direction of prayer and not knowing exactly what to pray in such a broken world. While this might be frustrating, Paul offers us some encouraging words in the midst of the journey to remind us that we do not voyage alone. "But the Spirit himself intercedes for us with groaning too deep for words."[23] What does this verse suggest? Prayer doesn't begin with me; it begins in the throne room of God, and we simply join in the conversation.

Prayer is returning to God what he began in heaven and what he practiced on earth. Even the very desire to pray is something God bubbles up within us so that we want to pray. There are moments when we are praying that we have no clue of what you should bring to God, but something comes over us, and we realize it's God praying through us. Sometimes it is simply a sigh or groan of agreement.

However, this is not an excuse for passivity when it comes to prayer. Though prayer does not begin with us, nor does it rest completely determined on us, we have the privilege of fostering it through actions of our will. Prayer will not happen to us. We will have to decide to create space in order to pray.

You are with Jesus in the School of Prayer.

---

22   Romans 8:26a

23   Romans 8:26b

I encourage you to begin the next few days with the following morning prayer or something similar from your own words.

Heavenly Father, I marvel that You delight in talking with me. I purposefully look for your promised presence in my life today. Jesus, as your disciple, I ask You to teach me how to pray. Holy Spirit, since I do not know how to pray as I ought, I ask you to pray through me this day. God, I am listening for you, and I commit myself to You anew. In Jesus, Amen.

Then walk through the day watching for opportunities in light of what you prayed. When promptings come, PRAY! What do I mean? Just keep talking with God. Become attentive to what God does between that morning and evening prayer.

Then, bring the day to completion with the following evening prayer:

Lord, I look back on this day with thanksgiving. I am grateful for the places where I saw your presence so clearly. I ask for your forgiveness for the moments where I tuned you out. If you want to speak to me in the night, I am listening. I ask for your peace and rest so that I would be renewed in strength and awake with courage for a new day. In Jesus, Amen.

15

THE LORD'S PRAYER—A MODEL
TO GROW INTO AND OUT OF

First, Thy name, Thy kingdom, Thy will; then, give us, forgive us, lead us, deliver us. The lesson is of more importance than we think. In true worship the Father must be first, must be all.

—ANDREW MURRAY[1]

The attention at the beginning of these petitions is on the exaltation of God and His concerns. In the initial phrases of the Lord's Prayer, Jesus fixes our gaze not on ourselves but on God.

—R.C. SPROUL[2]

THERE ARE THREE SOURCES from Jesus' life to help us in our apprenticeship on prayer. The first and second come from his

---

1   Murray, *Lord Teach Us to Pray*, p.26

2   Sproul, in *The Prayer of the Lord*, as quoted on GoodReads.com

practice, from descriptions of Jesus as pray-er and from those prayers of his that were recorded. Third, we have his teaching on prayer.

Jesus was vocal about the importance of prayer. In speaking about future tribulation, he called his disciples to "alertness and prayer."[3] He warned his inner circle in the Garden of Gethsemane to pray so that they would not fall into temptation.[4] He commended constant prayer[5] and made it clear that the quality of one's prayer life preceded the kingdom of God manifestation.[6] Jesus' last promise to his followers was the power for witness through the promise of the Holy Spirit—an empowerment that they waited for in devoted and united prayer.[7]

Even with all these examples, Jesus' teaching and practice are best united in what we traditionally call The Lord's Prayer. It might be more appropriately called The Disciple's Prayer since Jesus gave us this model in response to his disciples' request. Prayers such as the great High Priestly Prayer[8] or the Gethsemane Prayer[9] might be better examples to call the Lord's Prayer. The early church often referred to the Lord's Prayer as the Abba Prayer. Whatever the name, it has become

---

3   Luke 21:36

4   Luke 22:40,46

5   Luke 18:1

6   Mark 9:29

7   Acts 1–2

8   John 17

9   Mark 14

our "go-to" prayer in the church and so it is our starting point.

The historical and universal church has used this short prayer as a form of recitation. It is valuable in this form alone, as seen in the story of Todd Beamer at the beginning of Part II, but it can also be a model to be expanded.

The prayer has a clear flow that points to different aspects of prayer: praise, intercession, supplication, confession, and warfare. It moves us from mere transactional praying to full-orbed praying. Jesus uses an economy of words, which makes the prayer simple to memorize, yet at the same time there is profoundness and richness of the few words and phraseology.

Having served in France, Mali, and the United States; I have learned the Lord's Prayer in three languages. I observed new converts in Mali finding revelation in the freshly learned content. I have also watched people fly through the prayer in recitation without second thought. If we are honest, with ritual or repetition, sometimes we can lose connection to the meaning, but detachment does not have to be the end result of familiarity. I once served a church where the slower pace and intensity of the recitation of the Lord's Prayer each Sunday made it feel at times like the roof of the sanctuary had opened to the heavens.

We can choose to pay attention in the recitation. We can explore the depths of each phrase to know the deep themes that are flowing out of our prayer. I find that there is something powerful in knowing that the prayer has been offered to God billions of times in history and by millions of people around the world on any given Lord's Day.

Sometimes we need the familiar to launch ourselves into the mysterious and yet unknown. Also, we may find ourselves in times when our circumstances make it hard to improvise in prayer; in these moments, the Lord's Prayer can prime the pump.

St. John of the Cross, who had a mystical and yet complicated connection with God through Jesus, writes about the dark night of the soul when he could barely sense God's presence, let alone converse with him. During those seasons of his life, he felt like his prayers were bouncing off the ceiling and that God was silent in return. Many of us have experienced these moments. The mere recitation of a familiar prayer might be our best way to not lose conversational connection with God while we wait for the sense of the manifest presence to return.

Andrew Murray, who is thought of as a Dean of Prayer and who wrote many great books on prayer including the classic *With Christ in the School of Prayer*, speaks honestly about moments of dryness in his prayer life. He experienced many mystical expressions of prayer, yet he too experienced the challenge of separating from everyday life to get close to God.

Murray once critiqued the Lord's Prayer, dismissing it as a prayer for the less mature believer; for him, the high priestly prayer in John 17 is the real prayer. Andrew Murray is one of my favorite devotional writers, but I disagree with him on this point. When I pray the Lord's Prayer, with insights of each phrase and in light of God's action in this world, I am transformed and freshly attentive to the working of his hand.

Kenneth Bailey is a renowned Biblical scholar who went to the Soviet Union immediately after the ideological wall came down at the end of the cold war. As he was teaching pure gospel to people who had never heard it before, he kept hearing the same story. God had preserved his truth in that land even though the entire government machine was trying to obliterate it. He preserved his truth through hidden churches, praying grandmothers, and small portions of scripture that remained in daily liturgy.

Meeting one woman, Bailey asked how she had kept her faith. Her entire family were atheists; no one knew God. Every church had been obliterated in her area. Written scriptures were not available. The one thing the Communist government did was to allow the Lord's Prayer to be recited at funerals. The women repeatedly heard the Lord's Prayer as a child. There was something about it that kept drawing her to the God who was the object of that prayer. As soon as the opportunity arose after the wall came down, she wanted to find out about the God who was behind that prayer.

So, we might say that the prayer has power in its form alone. We should not be surprised as Isaiah writes that God's word does not return empty.

> *For as the rain and the snow come down from heaven*
> *and do not return there but water the earth,*
> *making it bring forth and sprout,*
> *giving seed to the sower and bread to the eater,*
> *so shall my word be that goes out from my mouth;*
> *it shall not return to me empty,*
> *but it shall accomplish that which I purpose,*
> *and shall succeed in the thing for which I sent it.*[10]

Praying the Lord's Prayer is literally praying God's spoken and written Word. Think about it: the Living Word spoke the

---

10   Isaiah 55:10–11

prayer into existence, and the Holy Spirit encoded it for eternal preservation. God's Word will not return empty. It has the potential to become his Word for this day as I pray it attentively.

Sure, the prayer can become as meaningless as any old wineskin. But the wineskin has the power when reinvigorated by rubbing the oil of the Holy Spirit into it. One way to reinvigorate the prayer is to revisit each phrase to draw out its rich meaning and then expand on the phrases to spontaneously personalize the prayer. Here, I summarize each phrase with one aspect of prayer. I will develop each of these aspects of prayer further in Part III of the book.

Our Father in heaven, hallowed be your name. Praise.
Your kingdom come, your will be done, on earth as it is in heaven. Intercession.
Give us this day our daily bread. Supplication.
Forgive us our sins as we forgive those who sin against us. Confession.
Lead us not into temptation but deliver us from the evil one. Warfare.
For yours is the kingdom, and the power, and the glory forever. Amen. Praise.

When Jesus gave us this prayer, he provided a diagram for us of fully developed prayer conversation with God out of the flow of his restorative desires for our lives and this world.

If you have not yet, memorize the prayer:

Our Father in heaven, hallowed be your name.
Your kingdom come, your will be done, on earth as it is in heaven.
Give us this day our daily bread.
Forgive us our sins as we forgive those who sin against us.
Lead us not into temptation but deliver us from the evil one.
For yours is the kingdom, and the power, and the glory forever.
Amen.

Pray the prayer out loud as slowly as possible, thinking about each word and phrase.

Pray the prayer, but stop after each phrase for personal amplification. For example:

"Our Father in heaven." Lord, this reminds me that you are close as Father and yet beyond my best imagination. As I approach you in prayer, I feel your welcome, but I do not want to familiarize you into my small provincial god. I bow my knee in awe. I sit in your lap in acceptance. Will you keep me alert to both aspects of your presence in my life this day?

"Hallowed be your name." Lord, you are revealed in many titles, names and descriptors in your Word. Today I celebrate you as Jehovah-shalom, the Lord our peace. I praise you Lord. I am reminded this morning that you still occupy the throne of heaven. And so, I choose peace today even though my world is filled with turmoil. Nothing can come my way except through the filters of your love.

And so on...

In Appendix 4 you can find a series of morning and evening prayers that coincide with various phrases of the Lord's Prayer. Consider using these prayers over the course of a week.

PART III

FULLY FORMED PRAYER LIFE

THE ANCIENT PREACHER DECLARES that God "has put eternity into the human heart."[1] What does it mean to have eternity in our hearts as humans? The simplest understanding is that we instinctually know that there is more to this world and our lives than what is obvious to the naked eye. There is an echo of a Creator, his design, and his conversation with us. This conversation was ruptured at the fall, but there is something in our human nature that seeks to get back to that conversation. Prayer is in our inner person, spirit and soul, and waiting to be embodied. Our whole being—body, soul, and spirit—is longing for this interaction.

Charles Haddon Spurgeon, a great nineteenth-century preacher from England, stated this inner longing in the following way:

> To seek aid in time of distress from a supernatural Being is an instinct of human nature. I believe in the truthfulness of this instinct, and that man prays because there is something

---

1   Ecclesiastes 3:11 in the New American Standard Bible

in prayer. As when the Creator gives His creature the power of thirst, it is because water exists to meet its thirst; and as when He creates hunger there is food to correspond to the appetite; so when He inclines men to pray it is because prayer has a corresponding blessing connected with it.[2]

Spurgeon experienced prayer as his lifeline. As a result, he is recorded as saying a number of times that he was so busy that he needed to get up a few hours earlier to profit from that time. Spiritually thirsty people must drink, and the call to prayer is an invitation to drink in the Lord. It is an invitation to address the eternity in our hearts.

Spurgeon is also said to have welcomed people to his London church who were trying to discern the secret of the church's success. He would lead them down into the basement of the church to a small room near the furnace. There, down in the depths, people gathered and prayed for intercession around the clock.

There are many ways to pray, and there are many components to prayer. If we reduce prayer to one component, we will miss the pleasure of a full conversation with God. I propose five components of prayer that are in the Lord's model prayer for his disciples that will help to enlarge our own prayer experience.

Praise. Intercession. Supplication. Confession. Warfare.

These components are distinct yet overlap. Praise can be a form of warfare. Confession and warfare prayer can be forms of intercession. The categories are not meant to be binding but guiding. By expanding our understanding of prayer beyond mere asking, we will enrich our experience.

---

2 Spurgeon, "Prayer Certified of Success"

16

PRAYER AS PRAISE

Prayer is that transaction, wonderful transaction where the wealth of God's glory is magnified and the wants of our souls are satisfied.

—JOHN PIPER[1]

The person of faith looks up to God, not at him or down on him. ...God is not a servant to be called into action when we are too tired to do something ourselves, not an expert to handle a specialized problem in living. ...We would very soon become contemptuous of a god whom we could figure out like a puzzle or learn to use like a tool.

—EUGENE PETERSON[2]

PRAYER IS ONE OF THE MOST theologically profound things that we do.

Why? Because it is a worldview statement: **God is God and I am not.**

---

1   Piper, *The Pleasures of God*, p. 210

2   Peterson, *A Long Obedience in the Same Direction*, p. 62–64

Even the simplest form of prayer, supplication (asking), is a declaration of dependence on God. However, praise prayer sets the tone for all expressions of prayer. It is an act of alignment of our lives to our Creator and Redeemer. This is our first calling in life: to worship God.

The Westminster Confession of Faith[3] states our first calling most succinctly in question and response:

> *What is the chief end of humans?* To glorify God and enjoy him forever.

Sometimes in contemporary society, we have a reductionist view of worship. Sadly, we have lived with a sacred-secular distinction in modern times, which has reduced worship to Sunday and in the sanctuary. All of life has the potential to be worship. The ordinary of Monday morning or Thursday afternoon can be as much of an anthem to God as a Sunday hymn or praise song. We worship all week long in how we relate to others, how we work, how we witness God's presence and grace in our lives and our world. Sunday is merely a community capstone. Together we express praise for our Creator and Redeemer who has made the week of worship possible.

The writer of the letter to the Hebrews captures this blend of word and deed in worship-praise in two short verses.

> *Through him then let us continually offer up a sacrifice of praise*

---

3   Confession statements have long been guidelines for good theology and practice. The Westminster Confession has been an important teaching summary for many branches of the Protestant church around the world.

to God, that is, the fruit of lips that acknowledge his name. Do not neglect to do good and to share what you have, for such sacrifices are pleasing to God.[4]

Sacrifice is a worship word. There are two ways to bring sacrifice to God in these verses. Acts of love—doing good and sharing what we have—are worship expressions that please God. Spoken praise points to the One who makes the acts of love possible.

Words of praise to God are an essential part of the Word of God.

The Psalms are filled with expressions of praise to the Lord. These declarations were set in place to help the people of God verbalize an aligned life.

O Lord, our Lord, how majestic is your name in all the earth! ... what is man that you are mindful of him.[5]

I love you, O Lord, my strength.
The Lord is my rock and my fortress and my deliverer ...
I call upon the Lord who is worthy to be praised,
and I am saved from my enemies.[6]

Ascribe to the Lord the glory due his name;
worship the Lord in the splendor of holiness. ...

---

4   Hebrews 13:15–16

5   Psalm 8:1,4a

6   Psalm 18:1,2a,3

The Lord sits enthroned… the Lord sits enthroned as king forever.
May the Lord give strength to his people.
May the Lord bless his people with peace.[7]

Bless the Lord, O my soul!
O Lord my God, you are very great!
You are…[8]

Jesus began the disciple's prayer with words of praise: *"Our Father in heaven, hallowed be your name!"* This is worship-prayer. And the prayer ends with praise-worship. *"For yours is the kingdom, and the glory, and the power. Forever. Amen."* It is a declaration of God's worth. The model prayer is bracketed by Worth-ship—declaring God's worth!

The apostle Paul would regularly break out into spontaneous doxology—praise—in his letters. He would be addressing a specific need in the church and be so moved by the work of God in his people he could not contain himself:

Now to him who…
Blessed be the God…
Every time I pray, I give thanks…

We were created to give praise to God. Our lives are to be a reflection of his glory in our daily worship. We have the privilege of punctuating our daily-lived worship with voiced praise.

---

7   Psalm 29:2,10–11

8   Psalm 104:1

Sadly, praise is an aspect of prayer that many do not grow into. We sing our praise. We embody our praise when the church gathers. But we are not always comfortable in praying our praise.

So, what is praise? To praise means to commend the worth of something or someone. In our case, praise means to commend the worth of God. By nature, it means to verbalize. The psalmists call us to sing, shout, declare, tell, make known, and so on.

Praise can also be punctuated with actions such as prostrating, kneeling, and lifting hands. This embodiment is a sense of positioning oneself in alignment to God.

Psalm 37 is a perfect example of this positioning. The psalmist uses a succession of strong stances in attitude accompanied by actions that suggest finding one's life in the overflow of God:

> *trust in the Lord,*
> > *delight yourself in the Lord,*
> > > *commit your way to the Lord,*
> > > > *be still before the Lord,*
> > > > > *wait patiently for the Lord,*
> > > > > *and fret not.*

Praise is the verbal agreement to see God as the source of all. It is declaring his worth. It is expressing an inner commitment to live uniquely for his glory.

There are different aspects of worship-praise. I once heard one of my friends describe the differences in this way: praise is our response to God's greatness; worship is our response to God's holiness; and thanksgiving is our response to God's goodness.

I have often distinguished between the notions of worship as adoration or praise and worship as thanksgiving. I make this distinction because I think it is easier for us to thank God for what he has done for us but more challenging for us to worship him simply for who he is. To simply vocalize his worth based on character, essence, being alone is not a natural reflex.

I realize that the separation of adoration and thanksgiving is an awkward and somewhat forced separation, as we only know God through his revelation to us. It is hard to separate our experiential knowledge of God from what he has done for us. However, I think the distinction is important because we can slowly reach the point where we reduce God to his gifts. We then have a transactional relationship, which might lead us to worship the gift more than the Giver.

I regularly remind myself that God is worthy of my praise, even if he never did a thing for me. So, given what he has done for me, I do not want to reduce him to his benefits. Doing so does not work in our relationships with other humans, and it will not work in our appreciation of God.

That said, thanksgiving is certainly an important aspect of prayer. I am overwhelmed daily with God's goodness to me, my family, and my community. I express this to him repeatedly. I have found the combination of thanksgiving and prayer to be the best antidote to anxiety.[9] However, I want to focus on praise in this chapter because a proper understanding and practice of praise is one of the keys to victory in the Christian life, but we have not been instructed well in this area.

---

9   Philippians 4:6–7

In understanding that worship-praise is worthwhile in itself because God is worthy, we can also become aware of some of the impacts of worship-praise. Three distinct things happen through praise: alignment, spiritual revitalization, and release of power.

First and foremost, in praise we align our life to the priority of glorifying God. Praise of God places worth in its appropriate place. There are other things of worth in our lives—people, opportunities, God's bounty, and so on. Whenever the worth of someone else or ourselves gets elevated to a level that makes God's worth forgotten, we have entered into idolatry.

I am to love my wife as Christ loves the church. That means sacrificial and serving love. But if I idolize her and make my life-meaning about her worth, I can enter into a false praise that will undo my purpose here on earth.

I am to love my children with an unconditional love. But if my focus becomes to make them great, or if I am consumed with their success and comfort, I might make those things of greater worth than their creature design—to pursue lives that bring glory to God. I turn them, or their future, into an idol. And no one needs the pressure of being an idol.

I am to steward all of life, with its opportunities, gifts, and fruitfulness, to the glory of God. Opportunities, gifts, fruitfulness—these are all good things to be appreciated, but they can easily become idols when they become bigger and more important than God. The word of God commands me to have no other god before him.

Praise is an active way to recalibrate true worth in life.

When we praise, we spiritually place all people, things, and experiences in submission to the King of kings. Over the past few years I have repeated a regular mantra in my morning prayer: alignment for assignment. My worship-praise, thanks-giving, prayer, pursuit, and interaction with God each morning are all acts, accompanied by an attitude of alignment to his way, all for his glory. Once aligned, I then wait for his assignments throughout the day. By waiting I do not mean that I am pas-sive—my day planner is regularly full—it means that my life is not driven by that planner but alert to God's presence and moments for revealing his glory in the lives of others around me.

Second, praise is important because it restores spiritual pas-sion. Praise by nature lifts our soul up. My countenance sinks when my circumstances make me feel overwhelmed. As I praise and God takes his place on the throne of my life, everything else takes its proper place, which is not over me but under his feet. Joy seeps into the cracks of my inner person, spirit, and soul, as I celebrate the Lord.

The prophet Nehemiah declared, "The joy of the Lord is your strength."[10] Interestingly, he declared this after announcing, "This day is holy to the Lord." Alignment to the first priority—the holiness of God—leads to the release of joy and a restoration of spiritual passion.

For this reason, the apostle Paul exhorts us as Christ-followers to "sing psalms and hymns and spiritual songs, with thanksgiving in our hearts."[11] Then Paul immediately ties this praise-worship into the worship of our everyday: "And whatever you do, in word or deed, do everything in the name of the Lord

---

10   Nehemiah 8:10

11   Colossians 3:16

Jesus, giving thanks to God the Father through him."[12] This is all the work of revitalization of our spiritual passion.

Worship-praise is not an opiate to escape the real world. It is a call to punctuate our ordinary and real world, even in our attempts to address its brokenness, with acknowledgment of the One who is of greatest worth. Praise is upward focus in the midst of outward service. We get revitalized in both focus and service, but service without praise often leads to self-congratulatory or self-righteous people. Real joy comes in linking the two.

God does not need my praise, though it does give him pleasure. However, I need to praise God because it restores my spiritual passion.

The third consequence of praise is the release of spiritual power. When God is lifted up, the atmosphere changes. There are several moments in scripture where the praise of God immediately preceded the release of power for victory in the lives of God's children.

One of the greatest stories is that of Jehoshaphat and his choir-led army.[13] In that story, the people of God were under attack from three allied nations. Defeat looked imminent. Jehoshaphat was afraid and set his face to seek the Lord. The Lord's response was unexpected: "Yes, there is a great horde before you, but do not be afraid as the battle belongs to the Lord." The battle plan was to send the choir in front of the army. The results were stunning:

---

12   Colossians 3:17

13   II Chronicles 20

*And when he had taken counsel with the people, he appointed those who were to sing to the L*ORD *and praise him in holy attire, as they went before the army, and say,*

*'Give thanks to the L*ORD, *for his steadfast love endures forever.'*

*And when they began to sing and praise, the L*ORD *set an ambush against the men of Ammon, Moab, and Mount Seir, who had come against Judah, so that they were routed.*[14]

Praise preceded the victory of the Lord.

Another interesting moment of praise unleashing a miracle was during the time when Paul and Silas were in Philippi. They were there as part of God's plan for that city, but God works in mysterious ways. Paul and Silas were jailed in an inner prison with their feet fastened in stocks. I would have been discouraged, would have second-guessed whether I had heard God's guidance correctly, and even would have been complaining. But the response of Paul and Silas to their plight was unexpected.

About midnight Paul and Silas were praying and singing hymns to God, and the prisoners were listening to them, and suddenly there was a great earthquake, so that the foundations of the prison were shaken. And immediately all the doors were opened, and everyone's bonds were unfastened.[15]

---

14   II Chronicles 20:21–22

15   Acts 16:25–26

We cannot say unequivocally that praise created an earthquake, but it is an interesting "coincidence." The result was not only the liberation of Paul and Silas (their comfort was not the real story) but, more importantly, the salvation of the Philippian jailer's family. As a result, the new church plant in Philippi took a large jump forward in one night of trouble and praise.

Worship-praise is worthwhile in itself because God is worthy. Worship-praise also has some clear benefits in our lives. As a result, I highly recommend it in our daily prayer lives. However, since it is not commonly taught, how do we grow in praise prayer? The following practical tools have helped me grow in praise prayer.

First, learn to pray the names of God in Hebrew. His names and descriptions in Hebrew celebrate aspects of his character. For example, consider some of the following:

Jehovah-jireh—The Lord our provider[16]

Jehovah-rophe—The Lord our healer[17]

Jehovah-shalom—The Lord our peace[18]

Jehovah-nissi—The Lord our banner[19]

---

16   Genesis 22:14

17   Exodus 15:26

18   Judges 6:24

19   Exodus 17:15

Jehovah-tsidkenu—The Lord our righteousness[20]

Jehovah-rohi—The Lord our shepherd[21]

Jehovah-shammah—The God who is there[22]

How does naming God work in prayer? If reciting the disciple's prayer, we might spend some time adding substance to the first phrase:

> *Our Father who art in heaven, hallowed be your name.* So. Lord, today I celebrate all that makes your name holy. You are Jehovah-nissi, the Lord our banner. You go before us. You come behind us. You are all around us. We feel safe in you.

We then can pray through all the names of God, building our prayer and praise.[23]

Second, we can allow the beauty of creation to ignite our imagination. Psalm 19 is one of the great descriptions of nature's beautiful reflection of God's glory.

> *The heavens declare the glory of God,*
> *and the sky above proclaims his handiwork.*

---

20   Jeremiah 23:6

21   Psalm 23:1

22   Ezekiel 48:35

23   See Appendix 2 for a list of names and scriptural references.

Day to day pours out speech,
  and night to night reveals knowledge.
There is no speech, nor are there words,
  whose voice is not heard.
Their voice goes out through all the earth,
  and their words to the end of the world.

Beauty in creation helps me to praise God. A palm tree blowing in the gentle warm breeze along the beach is my favorite space for praise-prayer. I write in my journal, as the trees clap their hands to you Lord, I life up my speech to exalt your name.

I do not have to be on vacation to find beauty. A woodpecker pounding away on a tree in my backyard or a butterfly flapping away to the glory of God can inspire praise. And I do not need to be in the more spacious and green places of suburbia or the country to find beauty. I have been moved to awe-inspired praise in urban settings as well. I've sat in a park and watched the masses of people passing to start the day. The beauty of God represented in that flourish of *imago dei* (his image in each one of us) has sent me to praise. I find the skyline of a major city or the architectural genius behind a structure inspiring. These are places of co-creation, where people took God's raw material, with his creative design in them and inspiration through them and made something beautiful. In those moments, beauty helps me verbalize my appreciation to my Creator.

Finally, it does not matter where we live, there is always a sunrise and a sunset. Whether those are reflecting off the distant waves, streaming through the trees of mountain grandeur, reflecting off the glass covered skyscraper, or peeking through a hole in the wall, the sunrise and sunset reflect God's glory. Pedro

Arrupe, a Jesuit priest, experienced this glory in a profound and unexpected way one day.

> Pedro Arrupe was visiting Brazil when, by chance, he met a very poor man who invited him to his home in a nearby favela. He had a gift for padre, he explained. So, Arrupe accompanied the man and was led to a shack, where the man lived with his wife and children. It was so rough, small, and spare; and it took Arrupe's breath away. He was moved so deeply, his eyes brimmed with tears. The man led him to a huge opening in the wall. Not a window but just a hole, and he pointed. It was a sunset. The only gift he could give was the view.[24]

Look up and out—be inspired by God's brilliance. Then, join the song and pour forth speech of praise in your prayer!

PRACTICAL EXERCISES

Try praying using the names of God as a form of declaring his worth.

Take a walk outside and allow creation to inspire praise about the Creator.

Punctuate each moment of pleasure during the day with a word of praise to God, who is the designer of pleasure.

When a challenge comes, or a life situation is threatening, give praise in acknowledgement of God who is bigger than all.

---

24   Boyle, *Barking to the Choir*, p. 154–155

17

CHRISTIAN

The prayer preceding all prayers is "May it be the real I who speaks. May it be the real Thou that I speak to."

C.S. LEWIS[1]

I BEGAN MY VOCATIONAL MINISTRY in a small church in New Jersey. Our method was simple: fast and pray; and attempt to be and speak the gospel in our community. As a result, our church grew with young believers.

We experienced a bit of worship renewal as well. As we brought glory to the Lord, his manifest presence became apparent. People came to church with expectancy. God released healing, freedom from oppression, with many people coming to a vibrant relationship with God through Jesus Christ.

We once had a young French man by the name of Christian visit our worship-praise gathering. He had found us through

---

1   Lewis, *Letters to Malcolm: Chiefly on Prayer*, p. 82

a friend of a friend. Without knowing the backdrop of God's sovereign hand, his path to us would seem rather random. During that worship service, he heard the Lord calling him into new relationship, in spite of the fact that he could not understand our English. After the service, he explained through an interpreter that he saw Jesus in our praise—not in the sense of believing through understanding but in the sense of visually beholding Christ himself as we sang praise. Christian's vision was a modern example of the King James translation of Psalm 22:3: *"God inhabits the praises of his people."*

Christian returned to France the next week. About a week later, we received news that he was killed in a tragic car accident. His arrival and experience at our church had eternal implications. God desires that all come to repentance, and he used worship-praise as the vehicle to rescue Christian.

We named our first son Christian. Whenever we are in a francophone part of the world, and I hear his name pronounced with a French back of the throat rolled r and nasal finish, I think of the power of praise.

Praise changes the atmosphere.

Praise transforms our hearts.

Later, as language students in France, we witnessed the release of physical healing during worship-praise. This healing was done not by the laying on of hands in prayer but by the healing presence of the Lord coming on people during the praise time. We have also observed the impartation of Holy Spirit freedom, life, joy, peace, deliverance, grief, and more during worship-praise. Praise often precedes God's victory in us.

18

PRAYER AS INTERCESSION

Self-will and prayer are both ways of getting things done. At the center of self-will is me, craving a world in my image, but at the center of prayer is God, carving me in his son's image.

−PAUL E. MILLER[1]

God's name, God's kingdom, God's will, must be the primary object of Christian prayer. Of course, it is not as if God needed our prayers, but they are the means by which the disciples become partakers in the heavenly treasures for which they pray.

−DIETRICH BONHOEFFER[2]

INTERCESSION AT ITS VERY CORE is to act or to intervene on behalf of another person. It implies advocacy. Some people distinguish between supplication and intercession in prayer.

---

1   Miller, *A Praying Life*, p. 142

2   Bonhoeffer, *The Cost of Discipleship*, p. 166

Supplication is described as prayer advocating for our own situation, whereas intercessory prayer is the notion of going to God on the behalf of someone else.

I am not sure that we can so neatly distinguish these two types of prayer. However, I will treat the next two phrases of the Lord's Prayer using these ideas of praying for others and praying for ourselves. I link intercession to the second full phrase of the Disciple's Prayer, "your kingdom come and your will be done," but it is absolutely correct to pray for the same for ourselves.

There are multiple images in the scriptures that capture the act of intercession. Each has a strong sense of earnestness. Paul refers to Epaphras whose prayer represented struggle or wrestling: "he [is] always struggling on your behalf in prayer... he has worked hard."[3] This is in the context of Paul's earlier challenge to the believers to "devote themselves to prayer."[4] There is an element of discipline and struggle in calling for God's kingdom to overtake the brokenness of our world.

In Genesis 18, Abraham pleads with God for Sodom. The narrative feels like a market scene as Abraham negotiates a better deal with God. The account needs to be read in light of what we know of God in other contexts. We know that God is not tight-fisted, a reluctant giver of mercy and love. So, what is going on in this story? Intercession is wrestling with God to prepare Abraham as an intervener with mercy and love on the behalf of others.

Another passage is Exodus 17 when the Israelites battled

---

3   Colossians 4:12–13

4   Colossians 4:2

with the Amalekites. Joshua led the army in the valley. Moses stood at the top of the hill with the staff of God in his hand. As long as his hands were held up, the Israelites prevailed in battle. When his hands went down, the Amalekites would prevail. Aaron and Hur assisted Moses by putting a rock under his arms and holding them up as he became weary. Moses interceded for the release of God's victory. Aaron and Hur interceded for and with Moses. Interestingly, in this account, God reveals another one of his names: Jehovah-nissi, the Lord our Banner. Intercession is calling for God to be out before his people—or rather, acknowledging that God is out in front of us.

A fourth passage is Ezekiel 22, where God through the prophet declares that he is looking throughout the land for "someone to stand in the gap." For what purpose? To pray on behalf of the people who had strayed from his blessing. Ezekiel describes the role of pray-er as a watchman on behalf of the people. The prophet writes,

But if the watchman sees the sword coming and does not blow the trumpet, so that the people are not warned, and the sword comes and takes any one of them, that person is taken away in his iniquity, but his blood I will require at the watchman's hand.[5]

Son of man, I have made you a watchman for the house of Israel. Whenever you hear a word from my mouth, you shall give them warning from me.[6]

---

5   Ezekiel 33:6

6   Ezekiel 3:17

The watchman of a city must remain attentive to potential danger in order to warn the people. Over time, the image of watchman was applied to prayer. In the case of prayer, when danger is perceived, the prayerful watchman must equally warn the people and call upon God to intervene on their behalf. This is somewhat of a prophetic role because often the danger is revealed by God, and it is God calling the prophet to intercede on behalf of the situation. There is a mystery to why God operates this way. My story of Amanda in Chapter 1 was an example of watchman prayer. God knew what was going on. He revealed it to me for prayer. He didn't need me. But my prayer somehow was wrapped into the story that he was telling.

The final image comes from Luke 18, in Jesus's parable of the Persistent Widow. In this story, a woman seeks justice from a judge. He eventually gives in as a result of her persistence, not necessarily on the basis of the correctness of her claim. Jesus implies in the words of the judge that the woman wore the judge out and he finally conceded.

Again, we do not want to push the parable to say something about God that is not consistent with what we know of him from the rest of Scripture. God is not a reluctant judge. The point of his teaching persistence is explained in Luke's commentary: "And he told them a parable to the effect that they ought always to pray and not lose heart."[7] Intercession is about struggling until we are ready to receive the blessing from God because his timing and way is always best.

So, what do these examples tell us about intercession? We

---

7   Luke18:1

are reminded that there is an aspect of prayer that requires waiting or tarrying to see God's intervention. In essence, this is part of our role in partnering with God in his restoration program. The process of waiting prepares us. But it is not just about preparation; somehow, our prayers are worked into the Sovereign plan of God for His kingdom release.

I like these three definitions of intercessory prayer from contemporary authors:

> An intercessor means one who is in such vital contact with God and with his fellow human beings that he is like a live wire closing the gap between the saving power of God and sinful humans who have been cut off from that power. The intercessor is the contacting link between the source of power (the life of the Lord Jesus Christ) and the objects needing that power and life.[8]

> When we pray for His Kingdom to come, we are asking Him to superimpose the rules, order, and benefits of His world over this one until this one looks like His. That's what happens when the sick are healed or the demonized are set free. His world collides with the world of darkness, and His world always wins. Our battle is always a battle for dominion—a conflict of kingdoms.[9]

---

8   Hurnard, *God's Transmitters*, p. 12

9   Johnson, *When Heaven Invades Earth*, p. 63

Intercessory prayer is an extension of the ministry of Jesus through His Body, the Church, whereby we mediate between God and humanity for the purpose of reconciling the world to Him, or between Satan and humanity for the purpose of enforcing the victory of Calvary.[10]

In each of these definitions, the point is about partnering with God in his restoration project through prayer. In the first, Hurnard emphasizes the intercessor's role in the release of salvation in the lives of needy people. In the second, Johnson emphasizes the role of kingdom release for the needy in healing and deliverance. In the third, Sheets emphasizes the role of intercession for connecting people to God and binding or blocking the work of Satan against people, all as the continuation of the ministry of Jesus and the ongoing release of his victory on the cross. Each author captures the conduit role—think of a pipeline—of the believer. It is God who brings the change, but the faithful prayer warrior taps into the power of God for this release.

Every person positioned in Christ has this privilege and responsibility to intercession. However, there is a difference in intercession as a task (privilege and responsibility) for every Christ-follower and the intercession of those who have a special grace-gift and calling to intercessory prayer. Peter Wagner offers the following definition of the Holy Spirit given gift of prayer intercession:

---

10   Sheets, *Intercessory Prayer*, p. 42

The gift of intercession is the special ability that God gives to certain members of the Body of Christ to pray for extended periods of time on a regular basis and see frequent and specific answers to their prayers to a degree much greater than that which is expected of the average Christian.[11]

Those who have this grace-gift can spend hours in prayer without any sense of tedium, and the time seems to fly by for them.

I have identified three types of intercessors. The first I call **Closet Intercessors**. These are the hardcore pray-ers. They go off into the woods for hours at a time or have a place in their homes where they lock themselves in for long periods of waiting on God. (Carl Tonnessen, to whom I dedicate this book, is this kind of intercessor.) These people can tarry long, waiting for God's release.

I think a biblical example of this type of pray-er is seen in Anna and Simeon in the New Testament.[12] They had been waiting on God and the release of his kingdom for years. When the baby Jesus was brought to the Temple for the purification rite, they saw the fulfillment of their long expectation in prayer. Anna had been waiting in the Temple "worshipping with fasting and prayer" for a period close to sixty years.

The second type of intercessor I call **Active Laborer**. These are people who have a strong desire to pray but pray more in the face of challenging situations than over many years. Moses was

---

11   Wagner, *Prayer Shield*, p. 48

12   Luke 2:22–38

an example of this type of pray-er. Moses' gifting and calling as a leader did not allow him the luxury to fast and pray in his prayer closet all day. However, on several occasions when he was facing a challenge, he would go off alone with God—the battle with the Amalekites, the receiving of the Law, for the healing of Miriam, for the Israelites as a people. His intercession was precipitated by the strategic point of battle or God's moving for his people.

The third type of intercessor I call **Target Intercessor**. These are people who neither spend long periods of time in prayer daily, nor pray broadly, but who might have a handful of specific prayer targets that they pray for over a long period of time—a wayward child, an unreached group of people, a person with a persistent illness, a missionary, and so on. A Target Intercessor may identify strongly with a particular need, which leads to a strong desire to bear the other person's burden for an extended time.

Now, please do not try to pigeon-hole people into my typology. These three categories are more descriptive than prescriptive. However, I have seen this understanding of types of intercessory prayer open up people to their forms of intercession when they are not the Closet Intercessor type. Moreover, some people combine characteristics of the Active Laborer and Target Intercessor. Maybe a description from my own life might be helpful here.

I am not a Closet Intercessor as I described this type above. I am far too active and filled with energy. My mind wanders too much, and I can lose attention if I am locked into one space or activity too long. This is one of the reasons I practice prayer walking and pilgrimage. The act of moving allows me to stay mentally engaged; it is also helpful for me to pray out loud. That said, I spend one to two hours every morning with the Lord. I journal, I write prayers, I read the Word, I read a chapter from a Christian writer, I write more prayers, I meditate, I process what I am hearing from the Lord. And during each season of my life I follow a different prayer pattern. Having an established pattern has helped me maintain order and direction for my prayer time, while continuing a more fluid practice as an Active Laborer and Target Intercessor.

For example, three years ago the Lord put it on my heart to pray for seven missionaries or missionary families every day. I followed this pattern daily. Then two years ago the list shifted, so now I am praying for eleven missionaries or families daily, including five from the original list. All have some level of engagement in my mission passion, and I have participated in varying degrees in their lives in the past. I am not certain why these particular people captured my attention but a sense of calling gripped me that I needed to pray for them daily until the Lord gave release.

Likewise, I have daily intercession requests for my immediate and extended family. I am like the Persistent Widow knocking on God's door. Why? Because he told me to do so! I do not think that my prayer is the essential piece. God is the first mover, the last mover, and the mover in between. I do not produce anything in prayer. But I do believe that I agree with his ultimate design for my own life and the life of others when I pray.

In intercession, we are agreeing with the Lord to overturn the kingdoms of this world with his kingdom. Though we are not producing his kingdom, to fail to pray could block or delay it. Jesus was straightforward: "You do not have because you do not ask." Maybe in those moments we get his permissive will rather than his perfect will? All prayer is ultimately lining up our will to the will of the Father. It is a Lordship issue. The Westminster Confession asks and answers the question:

What is prayer? An offering up of our desires unto God.

Thus, even when we are not sure what to pray, we can trust God to pray through us. The act of asking in prayer is a form of aligning ourselves to God's will.

Frank Laubach was a missionary in the Philippines. He learned over time how to hold each thought as a prayer before the Lord. It gave him freedom in intercession to not worry about the specifics when he was uncertain.

One need not tell God everything about the people for whom one prays. Holding them one by one steadily before the mind and willing that God may have His will with them is the best, for God knows better than we what our friends need, yet our prayer releases His power, we know not how...[13]

One of the questions I hear from students and parishioners alike is how do I know if it is God who is leading me to pray for someone or just my own compassion? I decided to eliminate that tension in myself long ago. Bottom line, if I have compassion, it is a gift from God anyhow, so why wouldn't I act on that gift? My lesson in this area came in an encounter with an elevator.

---

13   Laubach, *Letters by a Modern Mystic*, p. 73

I was a young pastor. One of my nieces had been hospitalized with unexplained seizures. We lived one hour away, so our initial support was by phone. It happened that I needed to travel to the town where she was hospitalized so I decided to stop by the hospital to pray with my sister-in-law and my niece. However, while I was there, I became aware of the story of a teenager who was a couple rooms down the hallway. He had fallen off of a cliff and had been in a coma for some period of time. My heart was grabbed by just the few details of his story. As I walked by his room, I saw some family members around him and I had this sense that I should walk in and pray for him and the family.

But then the mental gymnastics started. Is this your call, Lord? Is this just my compassion for what he has lost? I made it all the way down the hallway in this internal tug-of-war. I pushed the button for the elevator. The doors opened, I got in—and then I got out. I started to walk back toward his room, and then the mental conversation started again. What if nothing happens? Will the people blame God more? Is this just my inner sadness? I almost entered his room before turning again to walk down the hallway.

Elevator button once again. Entering elevator. Second-guessing. Exiting elevator. Starting back down the hall. Turning around. You get the picture. I was a faith yo-yo. I would like to say that in the end my faith gift won out, but truthfully, I left the hospital without praying for the teenager. The rest of the story is a reminder not to put too much confidence in our prayer or faith. That afternoon, the teenager came out of his coma. He started a long process of recovering a "normal" life after his accident. What would have happened to that family if I had gone in to pray? Would they have given full glory to God as opposed to being happy for their child's recovery? Would they have come into vibrant relationship with the Lord? What would have happened for the medical staff looking on? What if, what if, what if…

God is always telling the better story. It turns out that one of my friends was the youth pastor in town and befriended the teenager. The teen eventually came into relationship with the Lord. I do not know about his family. God desires that none would perish but that all would come to repentance, so he is not sitting in heaven with his hands tied behind his back waiting for us to help him. However, maybe my lack of obedience may have been a missed opportunity to take a few stumbling blocks out of the way for those looking on.

Shortly after this event, I decided to never again ask the question "is it only my compassion or God's calling?" Whenever a need comes before me that could benefit from a kingdom of God intervention, I ask the people involved if I can pray. I am not responsible for how God will respond. I am simply responsible to respond to situations that become potential places for his glory to land.

What about God's reputation? He is big enough to care for his own reputation.

PRACTICAL EXERCISES

Make a decision to initiate prayer in the face of any situation that needs an intervention of the kingdom of God. Ask God to give you courage to pray with people on the spot even through the awkwardness. Write down your encounter and wait to see or hear testimony of intervention.

Make a list of three areas in the life of your family, community, and church, where you want to see a God-breakthrough. Make a commitment to pray for these three areas every day for a month. Ask God if he wants you to continue praying at the end of the month.

Take intercession to the next level by partnering with at least two other people for regular intercession. Do this in person or via the Internet or phone. Watch and see what happens.

19

TALLY AND ANTHONY

Three times I pleaded with the Lord about this, that it should leave me. But he said to me, "My grace is sufficient for you, for my power is made perfect in weakness." Therefore I will boast all the more gladly of my weaknesses, so that the power of Christ may rest upon me.

—THE APOSTLE PAUL[1]

YOUR KINGDOM COME *and your will be done.* This is a prayer of surrender, and my experience has been that God's kingdom does not always come in the ways we might expect. Tally and Anthony's story is one of two individuals and a group of praying men whose lives became intertwined in a kingdom of God mystery.

Her name: Tally. Tally was a member of our church in Connecticut and attending university in California. Through a freak set of circumstances, including a poorly marked road

---

1   2 Corinthians 12:8–9

crossing and a fast-traveling vehicle, Tally was struck by a van and suffered a brain injury.

Her life hung in the balance. We did everything we could think of to support Tally and her faith-filled warrior mom, Mauri. We prayed and we prayed and we prayed. Ingrid and I even flew to California to be present and pray in person.

Tally miraculously held on to life and returned to Connecticut after uncountable procedures and rehab in California and New York City. Tally did not recover her full physical self but she found life—working, walking marathons, and bringing her big smile and ready hugs to our church. It was not easy for her. She felt the frustration of not being her previous self, but courage kept her pressing on. And my repeated mantra of prayer with Mauri in our communication was "more Lord!" We were delighted with each advance, but we wanted more for Tally.

His name: Anthony. Anthony's condition was more mysterious. He was found slumped over the steering wheel of his car. Doctors did not know what had led to his unconsciousness, but his life, too, hung in the balance. I did not know Anthony as I did Tally; I heard of his story through a friend. When I first heard of Anthony's story, he had been in a coma for several months.

Our calling is to prayer.

When I arrived at our church in Connecticut, I immediately initiated several prayer gatherings. In the beginning months, we had prayer gatherings at noon and 6:00 p.m. every Wednesday. A young man came to me and explained that his work would not allow him to attend at those times, and he asked whether I would consider having a 6:00 a.m. prayer gathering as well. I immediately agreed.

For the first gathering, the young man joined me and another man. The young man who initiated that time never came back, but the other man and I continued and invited other men to join us. This 6:00 a.m. prayer gathering continued for 11 years and was still active when I left the church.[2] The group varied in size, the setting changed a number of times, and some people came and went, but for a number of years there were five regulars who were there consistently in prayer.

In 2011, we were intensely praying for Tally and Anthony. Tally we knew more personally. Anthony was brought to us by Mark, one of the members of the prayer group, like the four men who carried the paralytic to Jesus. We were full on in prayer for both of them—we wanted to see a God-sized intervention.

There was a crucial moment during that time for Tally. She was in a hospital in New York City. So, we decided to take a field trip to the city to just be with Tally and Mauri and to pray in person for God's intervention and full healing in her life. When I suggested it to the men in the group, Mark reminded me that Anthony was in the same hospital. So, he reached out to the family to see if they would be agree to us stopping by and praying for Anthony.

Here is the e-mail that I sent to some of the intercessors in the church to join us in spiritual covering and to even consider going on the field trip with us.

---

2   Funny side note: At the same time, a man in the church asked me to start a Saturday morning, 7:00 a.m., Bible study. He, too, was limited to participate in other Bible studies because of his work schedule. So that first fall I launched a men's study. He moved to Florida within a few months, but the study he initiated continued for eleven years and still goes on today.

Chuck Davis <e-mail> to Prayer Team

Mon, Jun 27, 201, 7:47 PM

This Wednesday, my Wednesday morning men's prayer group is going to pray for h¬¬ealing for two people at Mt. Sinai hospital in NYC:

1) Tally

2) Anthony—a friend of Mark's who is in a coma. The family has agreed.

I will not explain all the details but it came about from our last gathering—we sensed a call to go. Healing!

I wanted to invite a couple of you to join us. We are already 4. I do not want to over run their hospital rooms so I would like to keep it to 3 or 4 more. If possible, I would like to have some women join us as it might be overwhelming to Tally and the family of Antonio with a group of men showing up.

Plan: leave at 3:30 pm. Pray with Tally 4:30–5:00. Pray with Anthony 5:00–?? Be on the road by 5:45 as I want to be back for prayer at 7:00.

Let me know of your interest and availability.

Blessings!

It was June 29, 2011. Our time with Tally was rich. There has never been a time when I have been with Tally that afterward I felt more alive because I had been in her presence. Though the enemy of our soul has tried to snuff out her joy, she remains a life-giver. We did not observe any immediate healing in Tally, but we had a long-term engagement in prayer, so we just kept trusting.

We went to another wing of the hospital to find Anthony. We were well received by the family. It turned out that there were already some people of deep faith around him. However, the news was not good. He had been in a coma for several months and was not showing any signs of coming out of the coma. The family was getting advice from the medical community to take him off of the life-support machines.

We went into Anthony's room, laid hands on him, and began praying. When we were done and pulled our hands away, his body jumped. He went back to a comatose condition and the medical attendant present noted that it was probably just a physical nerve surge.

But from that day forward, Anthony started progressively recovering. Each day brought new signs of life. Today he walks again, has a Facebook account, and has been restored to his family. From removal from life support to squarely alive.

We cannot prove that it was the moment of prayer that began to awaken him out of the coma, but it is another one of those odd coincidences. And it still does not answer all our questions. Tally was our main contact. She did not receive completely what we wanted—at least as we envisioned it. Maybe she received more and better but our vision is so spiritually near-sighted. But? Why not Tally? Why Anthony? How did

God work the intersection of Tally, Anthony, and four praying men, without manipulating the circumstances? And what better story is he telling that we do not yet see?

Your kingdom come—in your way; it is not always the result that I want. But I have no recourse but to trust.

20

PRAYER AS SUPPLICATION

Whether we like it or not, remember, asking is the rule of the Kingdom. "Ask and ye shall receive."

—C.H. SPURGEON[1]

"Dear God, thank you for the baby brother but what I prayed for was a puppy."

THE PRAYER OF JOYCE, A LITTLE GIRL

WHEN JESUS WALKED on the dusty paths of Palestine, he marveled at two things.

First, he marveled at the lack of faith. In his own hometown of Nazareth, his power to do miracles was limited by their unbelief. *"And he marveled because of their unbelief."*[2]

Second, he marveled at the completely opposite response—

---

1   Spurgeon, *Spurgeon on Prayer*, p. 109

2   Mark 6:6a

bold faith. *"When Jesus heard this, he marveled and said to those who followed him, 'Truly, I tell you, with no one in Israel have I found such faith.'"*[3]

Jesus commended bold faith. He encouraged it, and he responded directly to it. "Your faith has healed you."[4]

Jesus was so serious about asking in faith that he told us to ask **anything** in his name.

This type of access to God through Jesus scares us. I find that supplication prayer is one of the most misunderstood forms of prayer. This was especially true in a more affluent community where I pastored for eleven years. When I invited others to pray about their needs, I heard various versions of the following two lines:

"God has more important things to do than respond to my needs."

"I do not like to ask God for myself."

These responses might appear humble at first glance, but they are rooted in a subtle arrogance. They imply that I will take care of my needs and allow God to take care of other people who are more needy. *I got this one God. You care for the real needs.*

Supplication is just another name for intercession. The only distinction is that I am bringing my personal needs before God, not just the needs of others. It is really a relationship declaration.

---

3   Matthew 8:10

4   Mark 5:34

Paul Miller writes, "All of Jesus' teaching on prayer in the Gospels can be summarized with one word: *ask*. His greatest concern is that our failure or reluctance to ask keeps us distant from God."[5]

There are a few thoughts that can keep supplication, asking for ourselves, within an appropriate motivation or attitude.

First, we do well to pray in the full orb of the disciple's prayer. Praise, to keep God first. Intercede for those in our world in need. Keep his kingdom first and all these others things will line up. Confess, to be alert to the areas of your life where you are clutching to false gods.

Second, we do well to pray with an attitude rooted in thankfulness. People that appreciate the basics and acknowledge their source in God have a better chance against the insidious nature of envy, gluttony, and over-consumption. Prayer brings contentment.

Third, we do well to pray with hearts abandoned in submission. Jesus made his personal desires known to the Father. He was clear and resolute on his mission. Luke likes the phrase, "He set his face toward Jerusalem."[6] Yet the night before his very reason for being on earth—his crucifixion in Jerusalem, he requested three times for a different future. Jesus wrestled, but his final words were *not my will but yours be done*.

Fourth, we do well to pray with others. When praying in community, others can speak into our prayer life. Jesus noted an

5 Miller, *A Praying Life*, p.118.

6 Luke 9:51,53. After these two statements, Luke continues to point out through the rest of the gospel that Jesus was journeying toward or on his way to Jerusalem.

important manifestation of his presence in group prayer: "Where two or three gather in my name, I am in the midst."[7] In the prayers of others, we can hear Holy Spirit correction or guidance.

Finally, we do well to pray with a proper understanding of the nature of our relationship with God and how he wants us to view the gifts that he sends our way. I have found that four theological foundations can help keep my personal supplication in a proper balance.

FOUR BASIC PRINCIPLES FOR TRUE SUPPLICATION

1. Everything comes from God.

2. I am not my own, and thus asking means accountability to the Giver and responsibility toward others.

3. Daily asking demands trust in the Giver.

4. Daily asking requires contentment in how God responds, especially when his response is different than what I expected.

So, how do we move forward in supplication? I think we just begin telling God what we think we need and trust him that he will give us what we actually need. I do not want to

---

7   Matthew 18:20

miss something that God has for me by not asking; *"You do not have because you do not ask."*[8] At the same time, I want to grow in maturity in Christ, so I want to ask according to the principles of his Word.

The four basic principles that I suggested on the previous page help us to understand our relation to gift and Giver. To add to that, the following principles can be good guidelines for how to pray in supplication.

1. **Pray specifically.** You may ask, "But won't I be presumptuous in asking specifically?" We only receive on earth that which has been loosed in heaven, so I highly recommend praying specifically. John the Baptist said it this way, *"A person cannot receive even one thing unless it is given him from heaven."*[9] After you have trusted God with the general request, write down the specifics. I write numbers in specific prayer requests in my journal so when the specific request becomes true, I can glorify God more.

2. **Pray according to his will.** Romans 8 tells us we don't know how we ought to pray but the Holy Spirit groans through us. So, ask like Jesus: "Here is my desire God, but in the end, your will be done." In the meantime, when we don't know how to pray, pray *give us this day our daily bread.* Pray for the basics of your life knowing this is part of God's desire for us.

---

8   James 4:2

9   John 3:27

3. **Pray obediently.** Jesus said, *"If you abide in me, and my words abide in you, ask whatever you wish, and it will be done for you."*[10] One simple aspect of abiding is obedience. In John's first epistle to the church, he writes about our confidence before the Lord. John links answered prayer "to keeping his commandments and doing what pleases him."[11] When C.S. Lewis began his walk with Christ, he noted that he found it easy to pray for others, but he found it difficult to pray for himself. He said that this was because prayer has implications; to pray means that we will have to be obedient when God answers. When you pray, know that God may make you part of the solution to the prayer request.

4. **Pray persistently.** Jesus talks about this repeatedly: *ask*, *seek*, and *knock* all imply intensity of movement. His parable of the Persistent Widow honors and celebrates persistence in prayer. God in his graciousness withholds certain things because he has something better for us. At other times, he might delay certain responses to a better time because he is doing deeper work in us.

5. **Pray with fasting.** Jesus assumes that we will fast: "when you fast."[12] Fasting has a way of aligning my true hungers and desires so that God becomes everything in my

---

10 John 15:7

11 I John 3:21–24

12 Matthew 6:16–17

life instead of all the little things I desire along the way. Fasting makes us physically hungry, but it satisfies our spiritual hunger. I fast from pleasures in life for the sake of my soul, preparing and enlarging it for what God wants to do.

6. **Pray with the right motivation.** James corrects us for not asking and then for asking with the wrong motivation. *"You ask and do not receive, because you ask wrongly, to spend it on your passions."[13]*

The whole aspect of asking comes from Jesus' declaration to ask for daily bread. Physical nourishment is always a metaphor of the more substantial reality: spiritual nourishment. When we are living in accountable relationships, serving for the restoration of others, and doing all of this out of spirit of gratitude, we have established some good guardrails that allow us to ask boldly and with great expectancy. We can count on God to keep us on the right road. He will only give us what is good for our complete development—body, soul, and spirit.

PRACTICAL EXERCISES

Do a self-review. Where have you developed the wrong perspective on asking for yourself? False humility? *I should not ask for myself.* False security? *I ask only to attain but not necessarily to steward.*

---

13   James 4:3

Tell the Lord that you want to practice supplication in the way he intended and so graciously invited us to do.

Make a list of the desires that occupy the majority of your thoughts. What potential do these desires hold for supporting the work and restoration of the kingdom of God? At what point do they go off the path to become idolatry or simply selfish desires?

Tell the Lord that you want to abide in his fullness. Ask him for grace and power to use his bounty to bless others and to glorify Jesus.

21

KEN AND JACKIE

The harvest is plentiful, but the laborers are few; therefore pray earnestly to the Lord of the harvest to send out laborers into his harvest.

—JESUS[1]

GIVE US THIS DAY *our daily bread.* It is certainly appropriate to pray for daily basic needs. I could tell stories of work provided at the right moment; much-needed university scholarships; an envelope of coins saved for four years by a friend that paid off an unexpected debt at the precise moment. But there are so many of those stories. Since Jesus also said humans do not live on bread alone, a testimony of received living water and bread is more inspiring to me.

When I was serving as the Senior Pastor of our church in Connecticut, we had developed a special New Year's tradition. Individuals or families would come to the church mid-afternoon

---

1   Matthew 9:37–38

on December 31 for prayer and a New Year blessing. The format was simple: open sanctuary, open communion table, and a personalized blessing; no time constraints—leave when you are done. One pastor would serve the bread and cup. The other pastors were available to pray a blessing over the individuals and families as they left.

I also encouraged people to fill out a prayer request or blessing card for the year. Then, I would keep the cards to pray over them throughout the following year. I focused my prayer on the requests of the cards, particularly during the first two weeks of the year, and then would pray periodically through the year until I had a sense that it was time to return the cards to the people to encourage their faith. Below is the card for 2017.

```
          Thank  You For Coming Today.
      Please write down each person's name
          represented with you today.
    Pastor Chuck will keep cards to pray for
        a two-week period in January.
```

Stanwich Church

That year I designed the card to ignite the prayer expectancy of the church family to think of people whom they wanted to experience the love of God through Jesus Christ. On the back of the card, I suggested two places to pray into:

1. Where do you want to see the kingdom of God break into your life and the life of your family?

2. Is there a name of a friend that you desire to come to know God's love through Christ?

That year, I received close to fifty cards. The card shown above was one of those cards. On the back side of the card were five specific names offered for prayer request; people who the McArdles were praying to experience a fresh spiritual vibrancy. Two of those names were Jackie and Ken. Jackie is Christine's mother and Ken is her mother's second husband. At the time of the praying, Christine had not yet seen a lot of spiritual movement toward Christ in Ken and Jackie but writing their names on the card was a mustard seed faith act.

In July that year I returned the cards with the following note.

July 17, 2017

Ephesians 3:20-21

Dear Christ Follower,

I was hoping to personalize a note to each of you but I am not going to find time before the end of the month. I wanted you to receive back your prayer card from the New Year's Eve blessing at the half way point of the year. I have prayed through these cards about 6 times in the course of 6 months. Celebrate what God has done for you and press in to him while you wait for more of his blessing in your life.

Thanks for allowing me to journey with you in prayer!

Pastor Chuck

Recently, we were with James and Christine, and she reminded us of how the Holy Spirit moved in Ken and Jackie's lives after this season of focused prayer. When I asked Christine for permission to use their story in this book, she reached out to Ken. He added the following testimony.

From: Ken K.
Subject: A spiritual biography
Date: April 17, 2019 at 8:19:54 AM EDT
To: Christine

Sorry this is so long. Once I got started I couldn't stop.

I was raised a high Episcopalian (aka Anglo Catholic). As a child, I was immersed in daily ritual (Mass, Morning and Evening prayer) living a semi-cloistered existence for three years as a scholarship chorister at the Cathedral of St. John the Divine, in New York City.

When I left there I was back on the hard scramble streets of the Bronx with little faith to guide or comfort me, and only the memories of mysterious, beautiful rituals and the magnificent language of the King James Bible. My father died suddenly in front of me when I was 15 and what faith I had was woefully inadequate.

I had one brief flirtation knowing Christ in my teens after attending a Billy Graham Crusade. But for the most part my faith was ritual based and by the time I reached college it was dormant.

Throughout my college years I drifted toward secular humanism, which led to a deep disdain for all religion. I actively embraced Marxism and social engineering as a cure for the ills of the world. It didn't last; I found this perspective unsustainable as I matured in graduate school. I started to explore ethics with a new perspective, replacing atheism with agnosticism, drifting in and out of Unitarian Universalism.

I found myself on a renewed search for meaning in the context of religious practice. I was interested in Christ as a teacher and "good man" and looked to "liberation theology" for some of my bearings. In addition I studied Taoism, Hinduism and Islam. My fascination with Asian art and philosophy opened the door to considering Buddhism as a reasonable direction. I identified with Buddhism for a number of years and practiced meditation and a study of the Sutras. During this time Christ was a persistent presence and always a part of my landscape. I couldn't seem to understand why or shake His presence and I did try to distance myself from Him.

In time, I concluded that Buddhism was an inauthentic dead end as I confronted a meaningless world and faced internal and external challenges. I found Buddhist practice ultimately destructive offering me nothing of substance. I went to one of my old standbys; I filled my spiritual void with alcohol. In the despair of this haze I realized that there was probably nothing on earth that could make any sense or resonate with me. I knew I had a drinking problem and started going to AA meetings but nothing stuck. The idea of surrendering my will to God's was foreign to me, almost quaint.

Around this time, one of Jackie's sons suggested we go to a service at this new church in town, Eastpoint. I figured I would give it a try and tag along figuring it would at least be interesting. Thus began the most meaningful and important journey of my life.

I wasn't there 10 minutes before I felt the presence of the Holy Spirit. I quite honestly didn't know what hit me. All I knew was that I desperately needed it, and wanted to go back. Several months later I was baptized. Through the grace of God the past 2 1/2 years have been transformative beyond any expectation. I realize now that Jesus was beside me on every step of my journey and that he was not going to give up on me no matter how obstinate and misguided I chose to be. That's my story and I've never been happier or at greater peace.

Ken K.

As Christine forwarded this message to me, she asked for a fresh initiative to pray for a few of the other names that have not yet come into vibrant relationship with the Lord. She included these words: "I thought you would be blessed to know how your prayer card, my prayers, your prayers and other prayers worked together in his life!"

Christine went on to add, "As painful as my parent's divorce was for me, and how strange it is to have Ken in my life as my mother's husband, I see some cool weavings of the Holy Spirit. If Ken were not a part of our family, this introduction to the church could not have happened this way. Certainly I would not have been praying for him and would not have asked for your prayers for him."

There is no proof of correlation to prayer and result. Nonetheless, it is an interesting "coincidence" that spiritual vitality came simultaneously to a united, specific intercession focused on the kingdom.

It is also humbling. Not every request on the card was fulfilled in the prayer's exact desire during that year. So, we pray and we hold the results loosely. When we get what we desire we proclaim—praise the Lord! When we do not get what we desire we proclaim—praise the Lord! All gets wrapped up for his glory.

22

PRAYER AS CONFESSION

Our forgiving love toward men is the evidence of God's forgiving love in us. It is a necessary condition of the prayer of faith.

—ANDREW MURRAY[1]

Prayer is the constant calibration of the soul. It is a lifestyle of stopping and taking candid spiritual inventory. This is not spiritual paranoia, but rather the exercise of one who has a healthy fear of God and a sublime desire for glorious heights of intimacy with God.

—BOB SORGE[2]

PRAYER AT ITS VERY CORE is dialogue with God. Conversation. Relationship. And because God is Spirit, this dialogue is even more complicated than our human conversations, which are already riddled with unpredictability and uncertainty.

---

1   Murray, *With Christ in the School of Prayer*, p.79

2   Sorge, *Secrets of the Secret Place*, p. 19

Our relationships with others became complicated and conflicted at the Fall, which introduced animosity and frustration into our communication as a human family. This dissonance impacted our dialogue with God. God did not want to maintain distance. Even God's first move toward us to engage after the Fall was met with shame and hiding on our part.

So, God came closer through incarnation—the Son in the flesh. But that step closer did not solve the communication challenge. Jesus was regularly misunderstood in conversation by even his closest followers. How much more complicated is it today as we need to develop our spiritual communication skills?

Another element of communication breakdown is when we are uncertain of our relationship with God because of practiced sin. The Scriptures repeatedly remind us not to lose confidence or boldness in approaching God. Why? Sin reintroduces doubt into the relationship.

King David's prayer after his sinful failure is a graphic description of this breakdown. He acknowledged his iniquity, sin, and transgressions. He did not hide in self-delusion. But then he launched this impassioned plea in prayer, *"Cast me not away from your presence, and take not your Holy Spirit from me."*[3]

David—who is described in scripture as a man after God's own heart, as a man who inquired of the Lord, as a man who clearly heard God's leading—was left reeling in his sin, even in the midst of confession prayer!

The psalmist offers these words describing prayer: *"If I had*

---

3   Psalm 51:11

cherished iniquity in my heart, the Lord would not have listened.[4] Sin separates us from a holy God. Even after the chasm of that relationship is bridged by the grace of Jesus, when we wander off of his path, we will feel distance from God and uncertainty about the relationship. Shame is a natural reflex and induced, at least initially, by God's graciousness. Oddly, the shame we feel is a gift of spiritual grace if it makes us press back toward God. It is the convicting work of the Holy Spirit in our lives. The reflex of shame changes from a grace gift to a tool of the enemy of our soul only if we make it about our identity and allow the shame to become toxic. Sensing shame is different than being shame.

When other people point out sin, it does not always feel like a grace act. It can feel more like judgment, unless it comes from a friend like Nathan, who helped King David get back on the path. If we perceive God's presence as Overbearing Judge, we will feel that he is disappointed in us. No one wants to talk to someone who is disappointed in him or her. However, if we view God's presence as Corrective Grace, we will realize that he is not disappointed in us but disappointed for us.

We had a praise song at a church that I pastored that created a negative reflex in my spirit the first couple of times that we sang it. I liked the intent of the song, but it expressed a meritorious life more than a grace-created life. It was originally written with three verses that closed with the following lines:

Holiness is what you want from me.
Righteousness is what you want from me.
Faithfulness is what you want from me.

---

4   Psalm 66:18

I asked our worship leader to change the chorus endings to the following:

> Holiness is what you want FOR me.
> Righteousness is what you want FOR me.
> Faithfulness is what you want FOR me.

God is not in heaven wringing his hands, waiting for me to produce holiness, righteousness, and faithfulness. I realize that changing one little word might seem to some like nit-picking, but I think if relationship is not understood, we will find God more imposing than inviting. His disappointment FOR us is that we are missing out on these life-giving attributes.

He knows that I am created for those expressions—righteousness, faithfulness, and holiness. He also knows that I have a flesh bent against those expressions. He has provided a way in Jesus to have those grace gifts flow from my new identity in Christ. He knows that I cannot produce those qualities but has offered them to me as fruit of the Spirit. Yes, I must exercise my will to agree, but he is the producer of righteousness, faithfulness, and holiness in me.[5]

Confession is the vehicle in prayer that allows me to experientially realize anew God's welcome and presence. Where guilt, shame, perfectionism, and failure sabotage prayer, confession opens the way to unleash prayer.

---

5   The mystery is that, in my union with Christ, these are already my qualities. I am righteous, holy, and faithful through that relationship. These qualities are given to me because of the union. However, they become part of my daily activity by my willingly taking them on. The Christ-life becomes more and more my experienced reality through communion and cooperation with the Holy Spirit's work in me.

Confession is simply agreeing with God. Confession starts with naming my condition: I am a sinner. I need a Savior. Confession continues with naming my rebellion: I have sinned. I need a Sanctifier. When Jesus invited us to pray *forgive us our sins*, he is calling us to the ongoing restoration of the relationship.

Jesus told the parable of two people praying. A "self-righteous" pray-er thanked God that he was not like other sinners. A "sin-aware" pray-er asked God to have mercy on him. Jesus made it clear which prayer was more acceptable to God.[6] (Notice I said which *prayer*, not which *pray-er*.)

There is a habit in American positivity of suggesting that we will be okay if we just think rightly about ourselves. The outcome of this thinking is to imply that if I call myself a saint, rather than a sinner, I will act differently. I understand this notion. We act out our identities. But before I can call myself a saint, I need a dose of reality that I come into sainthood out of a condition of sin. And I prove that it was my original condition, even as a saint, by continuing to commit sins.

There is a Chinese Proverb: "The beginning of wisdom is to call things what they are." Sin is a real problem—not just the things that we do, but the condition that we were born in and fight daily. This is why I prefer *forgive us our sins* in the disciple's prayer, as opposed to debts or trespasses. Debts are repayable, and trespasses are misdemeanors, as we currently understand and use the word—but our sin is a death sentence. The apostle Paul, under the inspiration of the Holy Spirit, reminds us that

---

6   Luke 18:9–14

before Christ, we were dead in our trespasses and sins.[7]

It is God's mercy that our sin condition is healed (restoring our relationships with God) and in the process of being healed (as an ongoing practice of righteousness).

According to his great mercy, he has caused us to be born again.[8]

But God, being rich in mercy, because of the great love with which he has loved us, even when we were dead in our trespasses, made us alive together with Christ.[9]

It is God's mercy that our ongoing sin practice is forgiven. Notice the connection made between confession, the throne of grace, and mercy in the following passage:

Since then we have a great high priest who has passed through the heavens, Jesus, the Son of God, let us hold fast our confession. For we do not have a high priest who is unable to sympathize with our weaknesses, but one who in every respect has been tempted as we are, yet without sin. Let us then with confidence draw near to the throne of grace, that we may receive mercy and find grace to help in time of need.[10]

---

7   Ephesians 2:1

8   I Peter 1:3

9   Ephesians 2:4–5

10   Hebrews 4:14–16

When we understand how much God wants this FOR us (for our good) and not FROM us (out of our efforts), we are liberated to embrace the declaration that follows confession.

If we confess our sins, he is faithful and just to forgive us our sins, and cleanse us from all unrighteousness.[11]

Just? Yes, because Jesus already bore those sins on the cross.

Forgiven? Absolutely, and without question. In the words of Fleming Rutledge, "God submitted himself to the very worst that human sin could do; as our representative, he comes under his own judgment."[12]

Cleansed? Most definitely. This cleansing includes shame and accusation, the two tools that the Enemy of our soul uses to break down our relationships, both human and with God.

As a result of the relationship renewal aspect of confession, we may want to move confession up earlier in the prayer pattern. Jesus begins with God and ends with God in his model prayer for the disciples. Likewise, we too must always begin and end with God. But we might have more confidence in intercession, supplication, and warfare prayer when the major block to our confidence in prayer—sin—is taken away.

Lord, have mercy on me, a sinner.

---

11 I John 1:9

12 Rutledge, *Advent*, p.93

There is also an element of warfare in confession, which shows how all the aspects of prayer are interlinked. As a pastor, I hear a lot of confession. Actually, my wife and I have determined that we have a priestly anointing beyond the normal priesthood of all believers, as we hear confessions all the time. We have even had people we do not know just arbitrarily begin confessing to us in public spaces.

During counseling sessions when I am hearing a confession, I celebrate the process of verbalizing the sin. Why celebrate? Because what we bring into the light loses its power over us. We break the hold of the enemy and our own flesh when we acknowledge that sin still has too much space in our lives.

It is important in dealing with the bondage of sin to address the second aspect of confession in the disciple's prayer: forgive us our sins, *as we forgive those who sin against us.* Scriptures make a clear connection from our willingness to forgive others to our ability to experience forgiveness.

> *For if you forgive men when they sin against you, your heavenly Father will also forgive you. But if you do not forgive men their sins, your Father will not forgive your sins.*[13]

> *This is how your heavenly Father will treat each of you unless you forgive your brother from your heart.*[14]

---

[13] Matthew 6:14–15

[14] Matthew 18:35—Parable of the Unmerciful Servant

... forgive him, so that your Father in heaven may forgive your sins.[15]

... Forgive and you will be forgiven.[16]

Forgive as the Lord forgave you.[17]

... forgive each other, just as in Christ God forgave you.[18]

Jesus is harder on unforgiveness than Paul. Jesus makes it feel that our forgiveness is conditional on our forgiving others. Paul makes forgiveness a matter of imitation—since you have been forgiven so much, it should be a natural outflow to forgive others.

Jesus warns in another passage that a failure to forgive would impact our worship.[19] Paul frames forgiveness as a tactic of spiritual warfare when he warns us to *"forgive... in order that Satan might not outwit us. For we are aware of his schemes."*[20] In this context, it appears that one of the schemes or methods of Satan is to keep us in a state of unforgiveness.

John Bever has written a book in this vein, *The Bait of Satan*. In the book, he describes offense as the bait of Satan. When

---

15   Mark 11:25

16   Luke 6:37

17   Colossians 3:13

18   Ephesians 4:32

19   Matthew 5:23–24

20   II Corinthians 2:11

we take offense and do not forgive, it becomes an entry way or a foothold for the enemy of our soul. An unresolved foothold becomes a stronghold over time. When we fail to forgive, a bitter root can wrap around our hearts. The writer of Hebrews warns, "*See to it that no one fails to receive the grace of God; that no 'root of bitterness' springs and causes trouble, and by it many become defiled.*"[21]

Frangipane writes, "If we do not walk in a forgiving attitude, we will certainly become prey to an embittered spirit."[22] Unforgiveness is the foothold. Bitterness becomes the stronghold. He goes on to write,

> As long as you refuse to forgive, a part of you is trapped in the past where you are continually being reminded of your pain … until you forgive you will not be fully released to go on with your life.[23]

Our sense of being forgiven, being free, feeling fully released to God's purposes, is linked to forgiving others. So, we need to dive deeply into confession prayer.

---

21   Hebrews 12:15

22   Frangipane, *The Stronghold of God*, p. 98

23   Frangipane, *The Stronghold of God*, p. 99

Confession is best done on a regular basis. I call it keeping our accounts up to date with the Lord. However, if you have not made this your regular practice, you may want to go through an extended cleansing prayer.

Ask the Holy Spirit to walk with you through the stages of your life. Start as a child, then move through adolescence and teen years, into adulthood. Ask for him to alert you to unconfessed sin in your life. As you remember these sins, renounce them, reclaim that space as holy and set apart to the Lord, and reject any effort of the Accuser to bring that area up again.

Be especially aware of areas of unforgiveness. In the process of cleansing, you may become aware of areas that need restitution, the need to make amends for a sin you committed in the past against someone. Some sins do not require restitution and seeking restitution with others may even be more harmful than healing to those persons. I have observed some people transfer the pain of their having sinned to the person whom they sinned against. Restitution needs to be done with care and wise counsel.

If you have a trusted friend and Christ-follower with whom you could do the above exercise it is even more effective. What we name, loses power over us.

Remember, renounce, reclaim, and restore.[24]

---

24   I am indebted to John and Helen Ellenberger for the inspiration of this model. They called it 3R deliverance: Remember, renounce, reclaim. I have added *restore* (restitution) to remind me to avoid developing a pattern of cheap grace.

23

DONNA AND HELEN[1]

Blessed is the one whose transgression is forgiven, whose sin is covered. . .
For when I kept silent, my bones wasted away through my groaning all
* day long. . .*
I acknowledged my sin to you, and I did not cover my iniquity;
I said, "I will confess my transgressions to the Lord," and you forgave the
* iniquity of my sin.*

—KING DAVID[2]

WE ALL CAN RELATE to that nagging sense of condemnation
that makes us shrink away from God. However, his Spirit will
convict us of sin, not to hold it over our heads, but so that we
can come free. When we have wronged another person, we
naturally hesitate to approach them. The same is true with our
relationship to God. The resistance is not in him but in us.

---

1   Names changed to protect the truly spiritual innocent.

2   Psalm 32:1,3,5

My wife Ingrid and I have had the privilege of walking many people into God's open arms of acceptance through confession. Ingrid often leads seminars where she has the privilege of helping people find spiritual freedom. During these seminars, there may be a time of directed prayer when a person might become aware of wounds in their soul from sins they committed or sins done to them. As part of processing these wounds, participants can leave things at the cross, write letters to those who have wounded them to release them and then either burn or shred the letters, symbolically wash their hands as a way of saying I want clean hands and a pure heart, and finally have someone with flesh and bones to confess verbally. The invitation is to confess something they have never confessed to a person before. This is in accord with Scripture, as James tells us to confess our sins to one another to find healing.[3]

We have observed over many years of ministry that when people keep a secret and never speak things out with their mouths, that "secret" still has power over them. We often say, what we bring into the light loses power over us. Ingrid tells the following testimony.

> At one such conference, before I could even sit down at my appointed space for "listening to confessions," Donna, a woman in her early 50s, literally ran to me. As she plopped down in the seat, she said, "Finally, finally I can get rid of this secret. I've carried it my whole life and now I can be free." She confessed her secret to me, a living breathing human being, a sister in Christ, and she was free!

---

3   James 5:16

SPEAK UP! LISTEN UP!

Again, this confession is in complete accord with God's
Word.

*If we confess our sins, he is faithful and just to forgive us our sins
and to cleanse us from all unrighteousness.*[4]

*Whoever conceals his transgressions will not prosper, but he who
confesses and forsakes them will obtain mercy.*[5]

Ingrid goes on to give this testimony.

I have listened to confessions around the world, from a lost
boy in Uganda who confessed he murdered his neighbor
during the civil war, to an AIDS worker in Hyderabad, India,
who confessed choosing to abort their baby because it was
a girl, to pastors and leaders confessing pornography addic-
tions to affairs. A new freedom came to their approach to
God after confession.

One of my favorite moments in ministry was serving the
Lord's table to a woman who had not felt welcome for over fifty
years. She'd had an abortion when she was in her early twenties.
The tradition that she had been raised in told her that her sin
was so great that she would never be invited to the table again.
She accepted that as truth. I will call her Helen.

At this church, we believed in an open table; no sin was so

---

4   I John 1:9

5   Proverbs 28:13

great that the blood of Jesus could not forgive. At the same time, we took sin seriously and placed a high value on confession and repentance. We always consecrated the table and invited the people to approach after a confessional prayer and a pronouncement of forgiveness.

This Sunday, Helen sat in the back pew with her daughter, whom she was visiting. Her daughter was a regular, and she knew what we believed about the table. She took her mother's hand to go with her to the table. Helen refused and told her why. I do not remember if this was the first time that Helen told her daughter about the abortion, but she did tell her that it was the reason she was not welcome.

The daughter eventually won out, and Helen took the bread and cup for the first time in more than fifty years. Jesus' original words in consecrating the cup really ring out in this experience: a cup "for the forgiveness of sins."[6] Helen was beaming after the service. A fifty-year-old weight was cast off.

Forgive us our sins. The power of confession!

6   Matthew 26:27–28

24

PRAYER AS WARFARE

We have taken a wartime walkie-talkie and tried to turn it into a civilian intercom to call the servants for another cushion in the den.

—JOHN PIPER[1]

For we know that our defense lies in prayer alone. We are too weak to resist the Devil and his vassals. Let us hold fast to the weapons of the Christian; they enable us to combat the Devil.

—LUTHER'S *LARGE CATECHISM*

PRAYER AT ITS VERY CORE is an act of war. Anything directed by or toward God is an act of war because we are in enemy-occupied territory.

Our created purpose is to glorify God. Satan's purpose is to deface the glory of God. Satan "disguises himself as an angel of

---

1   Piper, *Desiring God*, Multnomah, p. 177

light"[2] to distract us from the true light. When we praise-pray we are striking at the very core of Satan's tactical arsenal because we are celebrating the true light. "The light shines in the darkness and the darkness has not overcome it."[3]

Part of our calling to glorify God is to be a part of the advancement of his kingdom. Satan, since his rebellion and his fall from heaven, has been building a different kingdom in the heavenly places.[4] This kingdom is in opposition to God's kingdom. The battle theatre is earth.

When we rebelled to follow Satan, we gave a footing for that renegade kingdom on earth. When we pray for God's kingdom to come, we are striking at the very strongholds that Satan has set up against the knowledge of God.[5]

Our provision for daily life is our inheritance from the King. Jesus made it clear: "Seek first the kingdom of God and his righteousness, and all these things will be added unto you."[6] This admonition comes after a long lesson on trusting God for the basics of life—food, shelter and clothes. Satan uses anxiety about daily provision to cause us to question God and undercut our trust in him. Satan even used this tactic in boldly tempting Jesus:

---

2   II Corinthians 11:14

3   John 1:5

4   The "heavenly places" is a technical term used by Paul to point to the realm of cosmic spiritual warfare. It follows the Hebrew notion of the heavenly courts where the gods did their bidding in ancient mythology. It does not mean that Satan is dwelling in heaven with God.

5   II Corinthians 10:3–6

6   Matthew 6:33

Come on, you are hungry. You have done well in your fast.
Certainly, you deserve some bread after such a long fast. Just
turn a stone to bread and enjoy.[7]

After forty days of fasting Jesus was naturally hungry. He
was accustomed to providing bread for others: manna to
wandering Hebrews in the wilderness, miraculous cake to the
depressed prophet Elijah, and the multiplication of bread and
fish was soon to come. Yet Jesus refused a shortcut for himself.
He waited on God.

When we pray for daily bread (and really trust!), we are
dislodging Satan's tactic to make us self-sufficient by replacing
Jehovah-jireh (the Lord our Provider) with self-jireh.

Our standing in God's kingdom is completely based on
God's work in us. We carry a passport to the kingdom of God
because of the work of our King.

For Christ is the end of the law for righteousness to everyone
who believes.[8]

For our sake he made him to be sin who knew no sin, so that in
him we might become the righteousness of God.[9]

Satan's tactics are to strike at our sense of confidence in
that standing in Christ. Satan is our adversary and accuser.
He is called the "devil," which means "slanderer." When we

---

7   Paraphrase of Matthew 4:3

8   Romans 10:4

9   II Corinthians 5:21

confess our sins in prayer, we take away his grounds of accusation. When we forgive and seek forgiveness, we break Satan's strategy of getting us to live meritorious lives, a system that breeds bondage to performance, rather than freedom in Christ.

Praise—upward prayer—is warfare.

Intercession—outward prayer—is warfare.

Supplication—inward prayer—is warfare.

Confession—inward and outward prayer—is warfare.

ALL PRAYER IS WARFARE.

However, there is a type of prayer that is even more offensive against the kingdom of darkness. I call it warfare prayer. It is full participation in Jesus' declaration that the gates of hell would not prevail against the church.[10]

Warfare is protective in nature. We run into the strong tower of the Lord and are saved. *Protect us from the evil one.*

However, there is an aspect of this type of praying that moves a step beyond the defensive aspect of the disciple's prayer ("protect us from the evil one"). This aspect is expressed in Paul's declarations of spiritual warfare: "We have weapons invested with divine power to demolish strongholds."[11]

I want to be clear at this point. God is always the first mover. But he calls us to participate in what he is doing in this world. Mark Batterson describes this call in the following way in his book, *All In*:

---

10   Matthew 16:18

11   II Corinthians 10:3–6

It starts when we get on our knees. Prayer is picking a fight with the Enemy. It's spiritual warfare. Intercession transports us from the sidelines to the front lines without going anywhere. And that is where the battle is won or lost. Prayer is the difference between us fighting for God and God fighting for us. But we can't just hit our knees. We also have to take a step, take a stand. And when we do, we never know what God will do next.[12]

There are some spiritual concepts that we need to understand before entering into this type of prayer.

First, we need to acknowledge that we are in a war. Sometimes our modern worldview, which offers natural explanations to spiritual realities, has made us unaware of the spiritual warfare that rages all around us. Even the term "warfare" makes some contemporary Americans squeamish. But to be unaware is to be caught unprepared.

Second, we need be alert to the war, which takes place on three fronts: flesh, world, and Satan's active dark kingdom. The apostle Paul referred repeatedly to our fleshly nature that is at war with the Spirit. He even described his own struggle with sin (Romans 7). So, the struggle is not just outside of me, between the worldly systems and Satan's kingdom that oppose God. The battle wages right within my own being. My flesh wars with the Spirit who has come to take dwelling in me (Romans 8).

Third, Christ came to intentionally "destroy the work of the devil."[13] He was clear about his purpose. His work of deliver-

---

12   Batterson, *All In*, p. 3

13   I John 3:8

ance pointed to the arrival of the kingdom of God in a new way.

Fourth, when Christ ascended to heaven to take his rightful place of authority, he commissioned us as his warriors in this battle. He did not leave us unarmed but gave us full authority when we were seated with him.[14] Our battle is not against flesh and blood but against a spiritual kingdom.[15]

Finally, we need to pray with authority, knowing the nature of the battle. Our enemy is fierce. He is stronger than us. But Jesus already defeated him and made a public spectacle of him.[16] Our task is to fulfill Jesus' victory because he who is in us is greater than he who is in the world.[17]

The teaching of Jesus on binding and loosing directly points to the active nature of warfare prayer. Jesus applied the notion of binding to that of overcoming a strong man to rob his house.[18] In this context, he was responding to the accusation that he was healing and casting out demons by the power of Beelzebub (Satan). He reiterated that his work was sign of the finger of God and a coming of the kingdom.

One day Jesus was teaching in the synagogue, and he saw a woman who had bent over and was unable to fully straighten herself.[19] This had been her condition for eighteen years. In Luke's

---

14   Ephesians 2:6

15   Ephesians 6:12

16   Colossians 2:15

17   I John 4:4

18   Luke 11:14–23

19   Luke 13:10–17

description of this account, the infirmity was the result of a "disabling spirit" (evil spirit). Jesus "loosed" her from the disability. When questioned about his action, Jesus replied, "And ought not this woman… whom Satan bound for eighteen years, be loosed from this bond…?"[20] In this moment, Jesus demonstrated what he had said in Luke 11 about the coming of the kingdom.

What is the prize of the spiritual war? The battle is for people and spaces that have been co-opted by the murderer and destroyer. Jesus made us ambassadors of his way, a way of life, liberation, and flourishing.

Beyond this teaching by Jesus, we see two explicit passages that point to the element of warfare in prayer in Paul's letters to the church. Paul writes the following to the church in Corinth:

> *For though we walk in the flesh, we are not waging war according to the flesh. For the weapons of our warfare are not of the flesh but have divine power to destroy strongholds. We destroy arguments and every lofty opinion raised against the knowledge of God, and take every thought captive to obey Christ, being ready to punish every disobedience, when your obedience is complete.[21]*

Paul moves our struggle beyond the flesh to strongholds that exist in opposition to the knowledge of God. For this battle, we have weaponry that is invested with divine power.

Peter Wagner writes, "Prayer is number one among the

---

20   Luke 13:16

21   I Corinthians 10:3–6

weapons of warfare."[22] I would say that prayer and the Word are the dynamic duo for shaping everything in our spiritual journey. The Word is our standard and also the sword of the Spirit.[23] Prayer is where we receive insight from God to understand that Word and where the Word becomes a "living word" to us as instructions in battle. The dynamic of Word and prayer together becomes a weapon to advance the kingdom of God. Paul's description of our armor brings the dynamic activity of prayer and Word together:

Finally, be strong in the Lord and in the strength of his might.

Put on the whole armor of God, that you may be able to stand against the schemes of the devil.

For we do not wrestle against flesh and blood, but against the rulers, against the authorities, against the cosmic powers over this present darkness, against the spiritual forces of evil in the heavenly places.

Therefore, take up the whole armor of God, that you may be able to withstand in the evil day, and having done all, to stand firm.

Stand therefore, having fastened on the belt of truth, and having put on the breastplate of righteousness, and, as shoes for your feet, having put on the readiness given by the gospel of peace. In all circumstances take up the shield of faith, with which you can

---

22   Wagner, *Confronting the Powers*, p. 25

23   Ephesians 6:17

extinguish all the flaming darts of the evil one; and take the helmet of salvation, and the sword of the Spirit, which is the word of God, praying at all times in the Spirit, with all prayer and supplication.

To that end, keep alert with all perseverance, making supplication for all the saints.[24]

Again we see the severity of our struggle. Our battle is not against flesh only but against principalities and powers. Paul exhorts us to be strong. He exhorts us to be alert. And three times he explicitly states for us to stand our ground. Then, he uses the imagery of battle armor to show that we are not exposed in the battle.

As we invade the darkness, we do so wielding the offensive weapons of Word and prayer. We were not meant to hide in a place of safety but to move out into this world with an active, warrior stance of taking back what belongs to God and what has been usurped by Satan and his minions. Henri Nouwen writes, "Prayer was no longer a passive religious event taking place in a sanctuary but an active, even dangerous and subversive act that challenged the very structures of the world."[25] All types of prayer are acts of war. Warfare prayer is a proactive stance of partnering with God to push back darkness. We should anticipate resistance from that dark kingdom as we partner with God in taking back what belongs to him.

---

24   Ephesians 6:10–18

25   Nouwen, *Discernment*, p. 147

Finally, here are three metaphors of warfare prayer found in the scriptures: Gatekeeping, Strongman Binding, and Veil Removing.

Gatekeeping: Ezekiel calls for watchmen on the wall. James reminds us to resist the devil, and he will flee. These two notions combine into the gatekeeping principle. There are spiritual gates all around us. Some are offerings of God's kingdom blessing. Others represent invasions of demonic destruction. In prayer, with authority, we close the gates to darkness and we open the gates to God's bounty.

Strongman Binding: Whenever I come up against something or someone or some situation that seems to be against the glory of God, I pray against that opposition in Jesus' name. In doing so, I am actively tapping into Jesus' invitation to agree with heaven in the binding of evil. It is a proactive prayer that declares and claims the victory of Jesus over that struggle. Likewise, I want to loose the kingdom benefits that have been already declared in heaven: healing, deliverance, and release from the impact of darkness.

Veil Removing: To me, warfare finds its greatest value in the liberation of the captives. We are reminded in the Word "that the god of this age has blinded the minds of unbelievers, to keep them from seeing the light of the gospel of the glory of Christ."[26] Only the Holy Spirit can illumine the eyes of the heart to make them open to God's love through the redemption of Jesus.

Given the heart of God, who desires that none would

---

26 II Corinthians 4:4

perish[27] and who desires all people to be saved,[28] praying for this type of intervention aligns perfectly to his desires. I believe that this is the most important place to invest my warfare prayer. I do not completely know how our prayers play out in God's work of drawing people to himself, but I find it life-transforming to join God in prayer for the liberation of the captives that I meet in the day-to-day.

God wants us to be active in advancing his kingdom as we take an active offensive stance in prayer. Because of the seriousness of this call, I must conclude this chapter with a warning. Warfare prayer is best done in community and with a growing sense of intimacy with the Lord.

First, **Community**. I find prayer far more meaningful in group than alone. The Holy Spirit has a way of directing a group in prayer that will take us to places where we cannot get on our own. I tune my ear to God in the prayer closet—in praying alone, just as Jesus did—but I hear God in unique ways when I am praying with other Christ followers. I find it amazing how the Holy Spirit will confirm something through the prayer of another or lead us as a group in a direction that I might not have gone if I had been praying alone. There is something about the power of agreement in prayer as well. When taking on darkness, I want the covering of being in the body of Christ.

Second, **Intimacy**. When it comes to warfare prayer and operating fully in our spiritual authority, we do not want to move out in warfare prayer at a faster pace than we are growing in our intimacy with God through prayer. To advance too

---

27   II Peter 3:9

28   I Timothy 1:4

quickly is to put ourselves in danger.

The model below is helpful to me to think about the correlation of intimacy and authority.[29] The vertical axis represents our growing in intimacy with God ("Holding God's Hand"). The horizontal axis represents our rate of engaging in active spiritual warfare ("Moving Out with God's Authority"). The ideal convergence point is when we are growing in intimacy at the same rate as the level of moving out in authority. We find ourselves in the danger zone if we are out in battle and cut off from communication with the Commander in Chief. Dialoguing prayer with God is where the ears of our heart are tuned to stay alert.

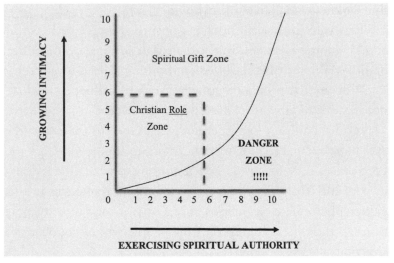

It is essential that we develop this conversation with God simultaneously with operating in our authority. In fact, it is the conversation that will create the confidence in our position in Christ and allow us to trust what the Father is saying and doing,

---

29   The model comes from Peter Wagner, but I do not remember the exact source.

and where he is going, so that we can join him in each.

I close with the following quote from Andrew Murray:

> Grant especially, blessed Lord, that your Church may believe
> that it is by the power of united prayer that she can bind and
> loose in heaven, cast out Satan, save souls, remove mountains,
> and hasten the coming of the Kingdom.[30]

PRACTICAL EXERCISES

What are the personal sin challenges that you regularly face?
What are the areas of your family or community life that feel
like darkness has gotten a foothold?

Pray with spiritual authority against the work of flesh, world,
and kingdom of darkness in those areas or struggles. Do not beg.
Stand. Make verbal declarations announcing Jesus as greater.

Who are the people in your network of influence who are
not in full and vibrant relationships with God through Christ?
Make a list and pray in agreement with God for their spiritual
eyes to be opened (II Corinthians 4:4). Simultaneously, ask the
Lord open a door for you to give testimony to what God is doing
in your life (Colossians 4:2–6). The biblical references in this
paragraph are here on purpose because you may want to pray
through the verses on behalf of the people whom you want to
see come alive spiritually.

---

30   Murray, *With Christ in the School of Prayer*, p. 115

25

SOPHIA

The primary way to overcome Satan is on our knees.

—DEREK PRIME AND ALISTAIR BEGG[1]

MAY 2012 WAS A GREAT MONTH IN LIFE. I graduated from Fordham University, earning my Ph.D. in the field of Sociology of Religion. It had been an eleven-year process. I had already completed my course work by 2005, but I then found myself amidst a departmental shift and a two-year dissertation battle.

Then, in 2007, God led us to a large vocational shift. I received a call to pastor a church in Connecticut. As Senior Pastor, there wasn't much time left at the end of 12- to 14-hour workdays to research and write a dissertation, so the dissertation sat on the back burner of priorities in my life.

Finally, I came to my deadline year in 2010; I had a year to finish. I am not sure what drove me more, a sense of responsibility

---

1   Prime and Begg, *On Being a Pastor*, p. 70.

and stewardship to not waste the previous hours and dollars invested, or my pride to not allow the dissertation to win. My youngest son launched me into a final dash to finish. His words, "You haven't finished that yet," landed like a fresh charge.

Thus, on my day off each week, I would travel into Harlem to attend various mosques and interview West Africans. My dissertation was on the social role of the mosque and masculine identity among West African immigrants in New York City. That topic is not pertinent to this story except to note that there was not much overlap of my dissertation and my day job.

Even with my Sabbath day free-time given to interviews and participant observation, I still needed time to consolidate my ideas into a cohesive written form. The only way I could do this was to work from 1:00 a.m. to 5:00 a.m. in the morning. So, each night before going to bed I would pray, *"Lord, you know how much sleep I need and you know how much I need to write. Wake me up at the right moment."*

It took a one-year extension to finish, but I finally defended my dissertation in January 2012. You do not have to imagine very hard just how wonderful that graduation day was for me.

The day was filled with pomp and circumstance. The university graduation took place in the open commons. It was a brilliant day. The university is so large that graduates were announced by department and stood at their seats to have degrees conferred in mass. Only the Ph.D. recipients walked to the platform to receive our diplomas. The doctoral graduates were then escorted to the next stage of our celebration at the University Church to be hooded and have our research announced. Again, the air was filled with pomp and circumstance.

Each student was pinned at the entrance with a metal

medallion before the ceremony began. We paraded in to glorious organ music as guests and friends looked on. Before we were hooded, the Dean of the School of Social Sciences stood up to give us a final speech. This is my paraphrase of her words: "The pin on your robe has the image of an owl, which is dedicated to Sophia, the Goddess of Wisdom. You will leave this university and pronounce a wisdom that is greater than any other wisdom." She went on and on, exalting this goddess of wisdom.

Finally, I could not stand it anymore, and under my breath I declared, "In Jesus' Name, I reject any association with this goddess of wisdom. The only Wisdom I pronounce to the world is Jesus." As I whispered this declaration, the pin, which had been secured inside my robe shot clear across the platform, landing at the other side of the stage.

What happened in that moment? I believe I was rejecting a curse to align with a false god, Sophia. Praying in my authority, in the name of Jesus, did not allow the curse to land. Interestingly, my 25-year-old son asked me after the ceremony, "What was that Sophia stuff about?" In his spirit, he discerned a false declaration in the words of the Dean.

Now, that said, I do not believe the Dean was aware that she was cooperating with a kingdom not aligned to the kingdom of God. Many times in our naturalistic philosophy and humanistic worldview, we miss spiritual movement around us.

When we pray for God's kingdom to come, for his will to be done, for his deliverance from the evil one, we are establishing spiritual boundaries. We are cooperating with God's better design for our world.

PART IV

FRIENDS OF PRAYER

PRAYER VIBRANCY. In my experience, very few people feel a sense of vibrancy in their prayer life. For some of us, it is a lack of experience and familiarity. For others, it comes from a disappointment in prayer that has not been processed well. For some of us, our lives are just too full. And if we are honest, many of us have little desire to pray.

Given the importance of prayer, this barrenness is sad.

I feel that we are in desperate times. Our society has become mean-spirited. Our culture is dominated by anti-biblical sentiments. It will take a spiritual revolution to turn this trajectory around.

Lives filled with prayer—prayer that is a vibrant conversation with God—will not happen naturally in this spiritual climate that we find ourselves. They will take intentional effort. As Jesus noted in his warning to the disciples about their prayerlessness, "The spirit indeed is willing, but the flesh is weak."[1] We

---

1   Mark 14:38

now live in a setting where the prevailing attitude is contrary to a belief in God or an expectation of his engagement in our world. Sadly, this sentiment has seeped into the church.

My calling at this stage of my life is to call the church back into the fight. The fight begins with prayer. The resistance begins with prayer. I am a living illustration to this reality.

Recently, I met with three different groups of leaders of church and mission. In each setting, one of the leaders remarked that they saw such favor on my life. Another noted that there was flourishing flowing from my past places of services. I have not produced favor or flourishing. These are the overflow of God's bounty. I have cooperated with that fullness through a life of prayer.

In my own prayer life, I have been boosted by some accompanying actions. I call these the friends of prayer. Over the next few chapters, I will recommend a few of these friends to you.

26

FASTING–A BIBLICAL
UNDERSTANDING

Fasting is still God's chosen way to deepen and strengthen prayer. You will be the poorer spiritually and your prayer life will never be what God wants it to be until you practice the privilege of fasting.

—WESLEY L. DUEWEL[1]

I was also led into a state of great dissatisfaction with my own want of stability in faith and love... I often felt myself weak in the presence of temptation and needed frequently to hold days of fasting and prayer and to spend much time overhauling my own religious life in order to retain communion with God...

—CHARLES G. FINNEY[2]

---

1   Duewel, *Touch the World through Prayer*, p. 95

2   Towns, *Fasting for Spiritual Breakthrough*

HER NAME WAS LILLIAN. She was a whip. Life had dealt her some hard circumstances, which made her a little crusty around the edges. I didn't know about inner healing when I started as a young pastor, but I wish now I could minister to Lillian with what I know now. Lillian loved Jesus. And we loved Lillian, so we just overlooked a lot of the crustiness.

During my early years as a pastor, we had a regular prayer and fasting pattern. We fasted one day a week, one week a quarter, and one month per year. It was not really a set program; I simply invited people to join me in my discipleship pattern of regular fasting. There were only a handful of people who joined me in regular fasting, but our intercession community kept growing.

One time we decided to fast for a week in response to a missionary need in our denomination. Our missions fund, which was collected to support hundreds of missionaries around the world, was running behind, and missionaries were going to be put on *pro rata* salaries. The denomination called for a special year-end offering to close the projected deficit. We agreed to take a special offering at the end of our quarterly week of prayer and fasting.

I rolled out an idea to our regular intercessors: What if we were to fast and pray for a week with a focus on missions? And what if we committed to give over and beyond our normal tithe and offering—the money we would normally have spent on food and any unexpected funds that came in during the week?

Two other couples and Lillian joined us in the faith vision to trust God in advance. We fasted for the week and met every evening to pray for a particular city in the world and for the overall funding shortfall.

Friday of that week, Lillian showed up at my church study. She was holding an envelope. She gave me the envelope and provided the following explanation. She had received some money due to her from an unusual source. I vaguely have the number $3,000 in my head, but it was so long ago that I have lost memory of the exact details. An explanation of Lillian's situation will give an idea of how big that amount was to her.

Lillian had been alone for years. Her marriages had been abusive. She lived in government-assisted housing. She received social assistance and did odd jobs to top off her funds. She drove a car that had back panels that flapped due to the rust. It was always on the edge of breakdown. She had medical expenses all the time. The amount in the envelope represented about four months' income for Lillian. She could have really used that unexpected offering.

She told me, "Pastor, I want you to hold this check and put it in the offering for me on Sunday. I made a commitment to the Lord that I would give any unexpected income that came in during our fast to the Great Commission Fund. I want to honor my vow to the Lord, but I do not trust myself to hold the check until Sunday."

I told Lillian that I was impressed with her integrity and that I would hold the check until Sunday but that I would give it back to her before the worship service. I wanted her to have the joy of giving those funds to the Lord.

Sunday came and we had a celebratory worship time and special offering. Lillian was beaming. She was part of the large global team that was taking Jesus' Great Commission seriously. No regrets, but absolute trust.

On Monday, she came into my study with some interesting

news and another envelope. Another government agency had sent her a letter explaining that her benefits had been miscalculated for a number of years and that she was receiving the enclosed check to make the matter correct. I again do not remember the exact amount, but it was double the amount that she had just put into the offering plate. This money would offer her incredible relief for her situation—eight months' worth of income.

Then, a second thing happened that week. A member of our church had been in the process of purchasing another vehicle. The sale was complete and rather than getting trade-in value on his car, he decided to donate to someone who had need. He had noticed that Lillian's car had back panels that were flapping in the wind. So, he asked me if I thought she would be offended if he just gave it to her. Lillian got a vehicle upgrade.

I like this story for multiple reasons, but the best one is that it cuts at the root of any health and wealth strategy for prayer and fasting or the seeding principle of giving to get more. Lillian was not thinking of herself. The letter with the larger check was sent before she gave the offering. She would have received it whether she gave the offering or not. What she would have lost would have been the joy of giving, which is a much richer personal experience than receiving.

Lillian was simply seeking the face of God. In it, she experienced his lavish bounty in giving and receiving. My theory is that you only get to keep for eternity what you give away in this chapter of it. The only name-it-and-claim-it that I subscribe to is "name my sin and claim my Savior's lavish richness toward me in paying my debt."

St. Augustine is quoted as saying in a message on Jesus' sermon on the mount, "Do you wish your prayer to fly toward

God? Give it two wings: fasting and almsgiving."

So, that we do not get the wrong impression of the meaning of fasting, it is best to begin with a biblical understanding of the discipline. Importantly, fasting is always used in tandem with prayer. Thus, it is connected to our relationship to God.

The Hebrew Scriptures note two primary reasons for fasting. The first was at times of crisis to mark a sense of repentance. The act itself was an expression of strong emotion or grief that was to outwardly mark some type of heart-cry. Fasting was often accompanied by acts of humiliation, such as the wearing of sackcloth and marking oneself with ashes. These were signs of grief and sadness in response to a bad situation.

Most often this repentance was a response in the face of corporate sin.

On that day they fasted and they confessed, "We have sinned against the Lord."[3]

Often in the face of corporate calamity or defeat, the assumption was that the people had brought the problem on themselves because of sin. So, they fasted to find God's favor. The people of God fasted after defeat in war.[4] Nehemiah fasted after he heard the news of broken-down walls from Jerusalem:

When I heard these things, I sat down and wept. For some days I mourned and fasted and prayed before the God of heaven.[5]

---

3   I Samuel 7:6

4   Judges 20:26

5   Nehemiah 1:4

Esther called the people to fast in the face of imminent danger.[6] Jehoshaphat called a fast for all of Judah to inquire of the Lord in the face of vast armies.[7] David entered a personal fast to plead for his ill son.[8] He called for a corporate fast at the death of Saul and Jonathan.[9]

In each of these situations there was a sense of desperation that drove the people to prayer and fasting. They desperately needed an intervention from God. Sadly, comfort can be a demotivation to prayer. In the situations noted above, the people fasted and prayed in desperation for God's intervention, and the result was hearing fresh direction from the Lord.

Jehoshaphat was given a battle strategy—although a bizarre one—after fasting and inquiring of God. He sent the choir out in front of the army. Nehemiah also received direction in the form of a call that gave him courage to take faith risks.

The people of God were also accustomed to community and publicly observed fasts. The Day of Atonement involved a community fast.[10] The prophet Joel called the people to declare a holy fast and a sacred assembly.[11] The underlying reason for the fast in each of these gatherings was a response to personal and corporate sin.

---

6   Esther 4:16

7   II Chronicles 20:3

8   II Samuel 12:16,22

9   I Samuel 12:21; II Samuel 1:12

10   Leviticus 16

11   Joel 1:14; 2:15

Another type of fasting in the Hebrew Scriptures was in seeking guidance from God. Moses fasted before receiving the Law.[12] Daniel received revelation from God for the interpretation of a vision while fasting.[13] God gave fresh vision in each of those situations.

Sometimes in thinking about fasting, we can create some false dichotomies between the Old Testament and New Testament practices of prayer and fasting. The idea is that the Old Testament faith was only works and the New Testament faith is only grace. Certainly, ritual without meaning is always possible, but we should never assume that ritual is always rote. This is why God warned the people about the meaning of a true fast and the pursuit of justice through the prophet Isaiah.

Is not this the fast that I choose:
> *to loose the bonds of wickedness,*
> *to undo the straps of the yoke,*
to let the oppressed go free,
> *and to break every yoke?*

Is it not to share your bread with the hungry
> *and bring the homeless poor into your house;*
when you see the naked, to cover him,
> *and not to hide yourself from your own flesh?*
Then shall your light break forth like the dawn,
> *and your healing shall spring up speedily;*

---

12   Exodus 34:28

13   Daniel 10:3

your righteousness shall go before you;
the glory of the LORD shall be your rear guard.
Then you shall call, and the LORD will answer;
you shall cry, and he will say, 'Here I am.'

If you take away the yoke from your midst,
the pointing of the finger, and speaking wickedness,
if you pour yourself out for the hungry
and satisfy the desire of the afflicted,
then shall your light rise in the darkness
and your gloom be as the noonday.[14]

I have heard people say that this shows us that God does not want us to fast, that it was just an old covenant idea that had gone bad. It appears in the day of Isaiah that fasting had become rote. Fasting had lost its primary meaning of heart realignment to God. A person or a community that is fasting to hear from God will hear God's love for the marginalized. So, the problem with the people in Isaiah's day was not fasting but the failure to act along with fasting.

During the period of time between the last events of the Old Testament and the arrival of Jesus, many of the Jewish revivalist movements continued with the practice of fasting. One such community was the Essenes. Many scholars believe that John the Baptist may have been a part of the Essene community. He was certainly aware of their community practices as his baptismal sites were near established Essene communities. In

---

14   Isaiah 58:6–10

fact, the gospel of Luke notes that John's disciples fasted often in prayer.[15] In Jesus' day, the Pharisees were also a fasting community. Mark's gospel notes, "John's disciples and the Pharisees were fasting."[16] However, this does not seem to be the pattern of Jesus' early followers. Jesus was questioned about the difference between other revivalist communities and his own. In the process, he did not abolish fasting but called his followers to think about it in a different way.

Jesus affirmed fasting by his action. His first act of ministry after being baptized by John the Baptist was to fast: "immediately the Spirit drove him into the wilderness ... [to be] tempted by Satan."[17] We know from Matthew's account that Jesus was fasting during the forty days in the desert.[18]

We observe two important lessons about fasting from Jesus' experience in the wilderness. First, fasting is not like a Christian talisman that puts us in a bubble against spiritual attacks. Fasting opened up the warfare scene and in fact was a significant aspect of the first temptation offered to Jesus, to miraculously produce bread.

Second, fasting might be the means to enter us into greater spiritual alertness where God's ultimate purpose is being formed into our lives. William Barclay observes, "During this time

---

15   Luke 5:33

16   Mark 2:18

17   Mark 1:12–13

18   Matthew 4

Jesus was fasting,[19] and a time of fasting like that necessarily heightens a man's mental and spiritual perceptiveness and awareness."[20] Jesus stood before an open door to ministry, and he initiated that ministry with fasting and prayer.

Interestingly, fasting was not his primary method with his own disciples, but he later instructs them to pick up the practice again after his departure. He moves fasting from rule to right, from legality to privilege, and from obligation to opportunity.

Jesus' most explicit teaching on fasting is recorded in the Sermon on the Mount. In his teaching, he appears to move his disciples from ideas of rigid ritual to the spirit of the law.

> *And when you fast, do not look gloomy like the hypocrites, for they disfigure their faces that their fasting may be seen by others. Truly, I say to you, they have received their reward. But when you fast, anoint your head and wash your face, that your fasting may not be seen by others but by your Father who is in secret. And your Father who sees in secret will reward you.*[21]

There are some interesting principles to help us here. First, he makes the assumption that his followers would fast—"when you fast"—even though his followers were seen as non-fasters in comparison to John's followers. Second, he brings the outward ritual back to a reality of the heart. The outward act is only a means to unlock or empower the inward transformation and

---

19   Matthew 4:2; Luke 4:2

20   Barclay, *The Mind of Jesus*, p. 34–35

21   Matthew 6:16–18

alignment to God's way. Jesus emphasizes that fasting is not to be done as means of gaining spiritual merit in the faith community but of turning our hearts to God.

I have heard people turn this notion of fasting in secret into another rigid obligation. Because of the emphasis of fasting in secret, some assume that others can never know that you are fasting. This was not Jesus' intent. He was challenging the institutionalized and formalized Temple piety of the Pharisees who fasted to be seen as more spiritual than others and as a means of earning some sort of spiritual merit badge. Jesus' point was about the heart (see also his view on public prayer in Luke 18), very similar to Isaiah's critique of the people of his day. As Dallas Willard is often remembered as saying, "The gospel is not opposed to works, it is opposed to merit gaining through works."

In another instance, Jesus was evasive in answering specifics on fasting.[22] He refused to lay down specific regulations on the nature or frequency of fasting. Living into and out of the Law was not meant to be an outward show but an invitation to find God's rhythms for a rich life.[23] In all things, Jesus does not abolish the Law but fulfills it and gives it back to us with his Spirit for our good. Man was not made for the Sabbath, but the Sabbath for man. I would say the same thing about fasting, prayer, tithing, and so on. They are all relationship-building, not relationship-establishing. John Piper states it succinctly, "Christian fasting, at its root, is the hunger of a homesickness for God."[24]

---

22   Matthew 9:14–15

23   Luke 18:12

24   Piper, *A Hunger for God*

As a result, the New Testament Church fasted. We have two specific instances mentioned in the book of Acts. In each case, it was a situation of seeking guidance for the future of the church, much like the practice in the Old Testament. Church leaders were worshipping and fasting when the Holy Spirit marked Barnabas and Saul as the first sent missionaries.[25] In the same way, Barnabas and Saul were fasting when they appointed and committed elders for the new church in Lystra.[26] Even though there are no further references to fasting, we come to understand the importance of fasting to the church from the extra-biblical writing of the early church.

The church throughout history has had different seasons surrounding fasting and prayer. Oddly, the more comfortable our lifestyles, the harder it is to embrace this level of abstinence. Societies with greater levels of dissonance and deprivation have a greater inclination to prayer and to fasting. This is often evident in the urgency and quality of their prayer life. Those of us in comfortable societies need to embrace fasting to cut at the spirit of narcissism. The spirit of narcissism will lead us to become lovers of ourselves and not of God.

Following the biblical examples, there seem to be two strong motivations to fasting: repentance and guidance. At the core of each is a heart-alignment to the way of God.

---

25   Acts 13:1–3

26   Acts 14:23

PRACTICAL EXERCISE

After having followed this biblical description of fasting, what questions come to mind? Write them down. You will find responses to common questions in the next chapter with practical suggestions about fasting and prayer.

Ask the Lord to give you a spiritual healthy and liberating view of fasting, prayer, and all the habits of grace. These are God's gifts to us.

27

FASTING—SOME PRACTICAL GUIDELINES

We do not naturally or easily shift from the mind-set of "getting and spending" into a mindset that sees Jesus as more desirable than the "sordid boon" of this world. … The point of fasting is to express longing for Christ and all that God is for us in him … to be satisfied in God alone!

—JOHN PIPER[1]

If you say I will fast when God lays it on me, you never will. You are too cold and indifferent. Take the yoke upon you.

—DWIGHT L. MOODY [2]

IT IS EASY FOR THE CHURCH to turn fasting into a meaningless and rigid practice. One of our earliest Christian documents is

---

1   Piper, *When I Don't Desire God*, p.170–171

2   Towns, *Fasting for Spiritual Breakthrough*

called the *Didache*, or the Teaching. Most scholars date it to the end of the first century. It gives a detailed explanation of many of the practices of the early church, including instructions on fasting.

Didache 8:1 reads, "Do not fast like the pagans on Tuesday and Thursday but on Wednesday and Friday." Tuesday and Thursday were the days of fasting for the Pharisees. Though this rule gives insight that fasting was important to the early church, it is an odd interpretation or application of Jesus' instructions. When Jesus challenged the Pharisees' way of fasting, it had nothing to do with the day of the fast but the intention of the heart. *Didache* 8:1 is a reminder that we are always just one step away from recreating a new "old" wineskin by getting caught up in the form than the function of the practice.

Given Jesus' warnings about the correct manner to fast and the early church's confusion, at times it is good to have some practical guidelines to fasting. I suggest the following principles of fasting that might help us keep from turning the practice into a rote activity or a new "old" wineskin, which cannot hold the fresh wine of the Spirit.

First, fasting is not an effort to gain a spiritual merit badge. The kingdom of God is not a meritocratic system. It is a grace system. Every aspect of prayer is a form of begging. We do not earn spiritual points with our prayer or our fasting. For this reason, I prefer to refer to fasting as a habit of grace versus a spiritual discipline. Yes, it requires discipline to do anything worthwhile (except maybe breathing). However, discipline can take on a tone of striving or self-attainment. A habit that becomes a place for the manifestation or appropriation of God's grace seems to be truer to the biblical description of a growing and practiced spirituality.

Second, fasting is not an advanced stage of begging God. We do not make prayer—intercession or supplication—any more powerful because we have fasted. Fasting is more about aligning our hearts and preparing ourselves to receive what God has for us. It also encourages our hunger for God and his righteousness more than our slavish appetites for the things of this passing world. St. Benedict is quoted as saying that fasting is "trimming the soul and scraping the sludge off of life." The prophets capture this sense of realignment of the heart as they communicated God's distaste for prayer and fasting that is not primarily about relationship with him.

Do not pray ... Although they fast, I will not listen ...[3]

When you fasted and mourned ... was it really for me that you fasted?[4]

Third, in a similar vein, fasting is not a way of manipulating God to do my will. Fasting is at its core an attitude of repentance and humility. Humility does not manipulate but align—align to God's way.

so that we might humble ourselves before God[5]

humbled myself with fasting[6]

---

3   Jeremiah 14:11–12

4   Zechariah 7:5

5   Ezra 8:21

6   Psalm 35:13

Fasting is one of the many habits of grace that serve our efforts to draw near to God.

Fourth, fasting has a way of intensifying our prayer focus during especially challenging times and serious spiritual battles. In those moments, we are intently alerting ourselves to the warfare and joining forces with God. We need to regularly re-appropriate the weaponry in our panoply. Fasting is one of our weapons.

Fifth, it is good to remember that the simple discipline of the body is good for the soul. We are whole beings. When our soul is out of balance, it can cause our body to cry out. When our body is undisciplined, our soul and spirit can suffer. The apostle Paul was alert to the need to control our physical appetites for our spiritual good.

> *Rather, clothe yourselves with the Lord Jesus Christ, and do not think about how to gratify the desires of the sinful nature.*[7]

> *No, I beat my body and make it my slave …*"[8]

As contemporary Americans, we have come to expect the best this world can offer. We are by birth and practice consumers. We are conditioned to comfort. Fasting cuts through our attachment to the temporary pleasures of this world. There is nothing wrong with these pleasures in themselves. However, given our distracted nature in an overly stimulated world, fasting

---

7   Romans 3:14

8   I Corinthians 9:27

is a good discipline to turn our attention to the more important aspects of life.

The examples we have in scripture on fasting are primarily from food and water, with the one inference to sexual relations.[9] Often the Bible's accounts of fasting do not offer details about the length or type of fasts. The text often states simply that the people fasted. At times, more details are given: one day,[10] twenty-one days,[11] forty days.[12] This has led some people to develop a description of different types of fasts: the Ezra fast, the Samuel fast, the Elijah fast, the Daniel fast, the Disciple fast, the Jesus fast, etc. These are interesting descriptors, but we should not get bogged down on formal names or rigid forms.

Given the multiple things that distract us in the contemporary world, beyond the pleasures of food and sex, it is good to consider multiple types of fasts. Fasting is a choice to abstain from **anything** that might be a hindrance to prayer. Some people choose fasting today from certain forms of entertainment, social media, hobbies, verbal communication, or social functions. At one period in my life as a younger man, the Lord told me to quit playing basketball for a period of time. I realized that I was getting too much identity and worth in the practice. There was nothing sinful about basketball itself, but there was something sinful and distracting to my spiritual identity in Christ in how I was playing it. This aligns well with two biblical passages.

---

9   I Corinthians 7:5

10   I Samuel 7:6

11   Daniel 10

12   Matthew 4

Therefore, since we are surrounded by so great a cloud of witnesses,
let us also lay aside every weight, and sin which clings so closely,
and let us run with endurance the race that is set before us,[13]

"All things are lawful," but not all things are helpful. "All things
are lawful," but not all things build up.[14]

Another translation of this passage reads as "All things are permissible but not all things are profitable." So, God could call us to fast from just about anything—whether sin or any other weight.

Therein lies the key. Fasting is not so much about the length or the what. It is about a heart connected to God. The heart connected to God will hear his specific prescriptions for unique fasts in different seasons of life. As the key to prayer is relationship, so the key to fasting as a friend of prayer is maintaining our daily relationship with the Lord.

What we need to remember is that we will not naturally be given to fasting; it will be a spiritual movement. And though the spirit might be willing, the body is weak. Thus, we might benefit from programming a regular schedule of fasting to recover its value as we wait and practice toward a more natural heart response to God in all habits of grace, including fasting.

As I have taught on fasting and prayer over the years, I have had some questions that are repeatedly asked.

---

13   Hebrews 12:1

14   I Corinthians 10:23

1. When I fast, why do I have a harder time spiritually?
Fasting is an act of spiritual warfare. If fasting is primarily about aligning our heart and lives with the Lord's will and assignments for kingdom release, it should be assumed to be a struggle. The enemy of our soul is not going to remain quiet. Scripture describes him "like a roaring lion."[15] Satan fears Christ-followers who are living out fully God's design and purpose for their lives. The struggle does not mean that we are outside of God's will. It is the very evidence that we are cooperating with his purposes for us. Remember, it was under the leadership of the Holy Spirit that Jesus went into the wilderness to fast and pray—and there the battle began!

We have seen some amazing kingdom of God breakthroughs in our ministry through times of fasting and prayer. So, if you want unusual victory it will require some hard times of spiritual battle.

2. When I fast, how do I get past being distracted?
The disciplining of our bodies is a reminder of how much we are attached to earthly comforts and pleasure. The apostle Paul said, "I discipline my body."[16] I like the older translation, "I pummel my body." Idols and strongholds need to be destroyed. We are distracted because we have gotten too attached to earthly things. The only way to get past those distractions is perseverance. Reminder: grace is not opposite of work, it is opposite of merit.

---

15   I Peter 5:8

16   I Corinthians 9:27

3. Why do I not see responses immediately?
Fasting is an act of alignment more than an act of attainment. If my calling to a particular fast is for discerning his will or hearing his direction, the act of waiting increases trust. I am not sure it would be God's grace to give us immediately what we pursue. Sometimes guidance or insight comes quickly in fasting. The church in Antioch had such quick revelation.[17] However, sometimes the waiting is the gift. Daniel fasted and prayed for twenty-one days before he received insight.[18]

Daniel's example gives us another insight on the impact of fasting. There is an intersection of heaven and earth at the moment of Daniel's fasting. During those twenty-one days God was working out an earth-and-heaven breakthrough in the heavenly places. The prayer and fasting were part of a larger story that God was telling, and of which Daniel was not aware while fasting. My experience has been that my longer seasons of fasting only made sense months or even years later.

4. What is the best way to prepare for a fast?
Fasting is a spiritual act before it is a physical act. So, listening to God prior to a fast will be key to start with the right perspective. However, it is also physical, so preparing our bodies is simple wisdom, especially for longer fasts. In a long fast, we get to experience a detoxing and de-bondaging of our bodies. Healthy eating prior to a fast is wisdom. Start the process of separating from rich foods and drinks prior to the official launch.

---

17   Acts 13

18   Daniel 10

In the same vein, it is wise to come off of a fast slowly and with healthy care of the body.

5. Are long fasts different?
As I have developed a regular pattern of fasting, I found that longer fasts are actually easier than the shorter ones. It is the initial separation from food that awakens all the fleshly hungers in us. With each day of separation, our bodies realize that we can be hungrier for God than the things of this world. We can live off of the Bread of Life alone longer than we realize.

When I am doing a longer fast, typically 21–30 days, I enter the fast in stages. Days 1–4, I might still drink fruit juice to continue to flush my body of toxins. Days 1–8, I might slowly reduce my caffeine level to the point that I am not taking any caffeine in at all. I do this because my body will have headaches anyhow in the beginning out of a sense of deprivation of food. I want to slowly disconnect from the caffeine. By the second week, I will be on water alone. On shorter fasts, 1–7 days, I usually do not remove caffeine completely.

This type of staged fasting has been beneficial for me. By week two I find that I have unusual physical energy and alertness to the Lord. This alertness transfers to physical sensations of the world around me; colors seem brighter, sounds clearer.

I have not completed a fast without water. I drink water throughout to be sure that I am hydrated and keeping my body healthy.

6. What should I do during the fast?
I follow my normal schedule during a God-directed fast. The only change I make is to set aside times around meal hours to

press in to the Lord with more intense prayer.

I have fasted 21–30 days a number of times in my life. During some of those times, we were living in Mali, where the heat was oppressive and life was generally more challenging day-to-day. During one twenty-one day fast, I felt compelled to keep my running schedule every morning. I would run four miles per day. The Lord undergirded me with supernatural energy during those times.

You can read your own body. You can tune your own ear. God will give you both wisdom and direction on how to fast. If you enter this process training your body, you will be able to grow into this habit of grace. Start out with one day per week (remember that this will be harder in the beginning than when you get to a point of longer fasts), then try 3–4 day fasts, and so on.

7. What if I have a medical condition?
Please see a physician before fasting. Wisdom and discernment walk together as friends.

8. How do I handle the awkwardness of invitations to meals and restaurant meetings?
You can take the awkwardness out by simply being straightforward. Some invitations can easily be postponed. If a person is insistent on being together, then just explain that the Lord has called you to a season of fasting and prayer. Some people feel awkward about saying this because of the rigid interpretation of Jesus' words to not let our left hand know what our right

hand is doing.[19] His intent in those words was to keep us from taking spiritual worth from our acts. Avoiding awkwardness in love and maintaining relationships are not flaunting our works.

Other invitations cannot be postponed. An example might be a business meeting or a regular group gathering that involves food. Again, I suggest that you simply explain yourself and sit with the people eating. They may feel bad eating in front of you. Tell them that it is not awkward for you and that part of your pursuit of God is to relish in the blessings of others.

When we lived in Mali, our kids were younger and the mealtime was an important part of our family time. My kids were used to me sitting at the table not eating while they ate their meals. We are a playful family, so as they got older they would raise their forks every once in awhile by my nose in a jest of pleasure. Actually, during those times, I really enjoyed preparing food for my family as an act of service. The fasting can be a fun social moment when we simply make it a natural part of life.

How to avoid awkwardness? It begins with you. Be natural in the spiritual.

When I think about the times in which we live, I cannot think of any period in recent history where comfort and pleasure were so accessible because of our wealth. Fasting is a great way to remind comfort and pleasure that they are not our gods. At the same time, it points to the disruptive nature of grace that is needed in our day. We have commoditized God. Fasting is a way of realigning ourselves to a notion of God who is not just a supplier of comfort and pleasure.

---

19   Matthew 6:4

Ask God what type of fast would best realign your heart. When you have a sense of what this would be, establish a daily fast once per week. After several months of practice during which this becomes more natural, ask the Lord if you are to consider a longer period of time in fasting and prayer. Make sure that prayer does not get lost in the practice.

28

PRAYER WALKING

… praying for joy will be multiplied in its effectiveness when we think corporately. The fight for joy is a battle to be fought alongside comrades. We do not fight alone.

−JOHN PIPER[1]

Brother, if you would enter that Province, you must go forward on your knees.

−J. HUDSON TAYLOR[2]

ONE OF THE MORE RECENTLY EXPLORED METHODS of praying has been prayer walking. I have heard multiple other names for this type of prayer: mobile intercession, praying on site with insight, faith walks, and walking and praying.

I began the discipline of prayer walking when we lived in

---

1   Piper, *When I Don't Desire God*, p. 173

2   Taylor, *Hudson Taylor's Spiritual Secret*, p. 36

France. I began for natural reasons. We lived in a small apartment, and we had three children under the age of three. I would wake up early in the morning for my quiet time with the Lord, and if the kids heard me up and about, they would want to play. So, I would lay out my clothes the night before and sneak out of the apartment before they could stir enough to wake up. My practice was to walk with a small pocket Bible in hand. I would stop under a streetlight occasionally to read the next paragraph in the Word. I would then continue to walk, meditating on and praying that Word.

I began noticing things in the spiritual climate as I prayed. I actually had a couple strong manifestations of the kingdom of darkness against me as I prayed. I also received spiritual insights from the Lord about the places where I walked. Thus, my prayer was part intercession and part warfare.

During this period the Lord gave me Joshua 1:3 as a word of promise that I sensed I was to personalize for my life and ministry. *"I will give you every place where you set your foot."* I saw myself as proactively pressing against the darkness in the area as I took prayer to the streets.

It was later that a friend gave me this definition: prayer walking is intercession on location, with information, in cooperation, against opposition, for the glorification of Jesus.

It sounds very spiritual, and it is, but I became a prayer walker for natural reasons—I have an attention deficit. Therefore, praying while sitting quietly tends to lead to my mind wandering. When I walk and pray out loud, I have less distraction.

I like to have my quiet time on the back patio in the warmer months. Even in late spring or early fall, I might put the fire pit on, grab a blanket, and pray out in nature. Or I might go to a park to walk and pray. I recommend this type of prayer to those of you who have more active metabolisms or minds.

Another way to do a prayer walk is to walk together with other believers to saturate an area with prayer. I have practiced this as well. The Malians loved this type of prayer mobilization. We observed some pretty strong occurrences of power and miraculous intervention that followed a group prayer walk. I have used it with French and American communities as well to mobilize more active prayer.

How do I organize a prayer walk? I begin with a short teaching on prayer walking in which I emphasize the following practical steps or principles.

First, don't get over-religious and draw attention to yourself. In a group of two or three, you can pray conversationally as you walk. People who see you will just see you in conversation; they will not know that God is on the other side of that conversation unless the Spirit tells them.

Second, pray with the eyes of your heart wide open. Ask the Lord to reveal his heart for the area and the broken circumstances of the people living in the area. What does he want you to intercede for that is physically concealed behind the closed doors and drawn shades?

Third, know all of your divinely invested weapons of warfare and the various aspects of prayer. You will be praise-praying. A friend once commented about prayer walking, "I am going to a place where God is not adored and I am going to lift him up as Lord there." Praise changes the spiritual atmosphere. It will certainly be warfare prayer. We are in Satan-dominated territory. We are not to walk in fear, but we are to walk with alertness and with a sense of our spiritual authority, knowing our position in Christ.[3]

To keep focused in prayer walking, I also find it helpful to simply pray God's Word.

Jesus told us to pray for the kingdom to come.[4] As I walk, I pray for the aspects of his kingdom to overturn the kingdoms of this world. Life over death. Flourishing over poverty. Love over hate. And so on.

Jesus told us to ask the Lord of the harvest to send laborers into the harvest field.[5] I pray for spiritual alertness for those who know God in the area and a fresh passion to be good news as witnesses to their community. I also pray for the sending of new voices of good news.

Paul told the believers in Colossae to pray for open doors and graciousness in the communication of the gospel.[6] He also reminded the believers in Corinth that "The god of this age has blinded unbelievers to the light of the gospel."[7] I link these two together in intercession and warfare—joining God in pulling spiritual blinders off.

All of these focuses in prayer speak to God's heart for an area: he desires that no one would perish and all might come to repentance.[8]

---

3   If this notion of spiritual authority is not common to you, I encourage you to read my book *The Bold Christian*.

4   Luke 11:2

5   Matthew 9:36–38

6   Colossians 4:3

7   II Corinthians 4:4

8   II Peter 3: 8–9

I have had people object to prayer walking, since it is not a method found in the Bible. I find this objection fascinating. We do a lot of things in our faith journey that are not specifically mentioned in the Bible. My response is that I am not told to not do it either. Walking is not forbidden. Prayer is not forbidden. We are instructed to pray continually. Thus, the bringing of the two together seems to be well within acceptability of God's allowance for our lives.

I do not think prayer walking is more powerful than prayer sitting or prayer kneeling. It is like any habit of grace. The reason behind the habit is important. And any faith practice has the potential to become a new "old" wineskin or take on unhealthy magical or talismanic qualities. Prayer walking is no different than praying in Jesus' name. Jesus declared the importance of the practice of praying in his name.[9] However, in time that practice can become meaningless or even worse. In the story of the sons of Sceva,[10] we read of the unwanted results of prayer as magical ritual versus prayer as relational position. I refuse to live by the slippery slope argument that just because a practice has potential for misuse, we should reject it from the beginning. Everything good has the potential to stray off course and lead to frivolity or idolatry. Even so, I do not want to give away a helpful tool because it could be used inappropriately, and I have found prayer walking a useful habit to counter my attention deficit and to mobilize community prayer.

---

9   John 14:13–14

10   Acts 19:11–20

Set time aside to prayer walk your neighborhood. Follow some of the steps above. You can make some notes to keep you focused on an index card or on your phone. You could also write down Scripture to have ready to recite in prayer.

If you find the exercise meaningful or adding fresh energy to your prayer life, invite a friend or two along to join you. Sharing the process of growing in prayer is active discipleship.

29

PRAYER AND AGREEMENT

When God aims to do a great work, the first thing he harnesses is the power of prayer. He starts by planting the spark of desire in a few hearts. Then through prayer he gains it into a flame. Then the flame of desire and faith spreads to others. Soon large numbers are on their knees imploring the great work. Then God acts. Then he pours down his blessing. God loves to do great works of redemption. But even more he loves to do it in answer to prayer.

−JOHN PIPER[1]

Nothing tends more to cement the hearts of Christians than praying together. Never do they love one another so well as when they witness the outpouring of each other's hearts in prayer.

−CHARLES FINNEY[2]

---

1 Piper, "We Have Not Because We Ask Not"

2 Finney, "Lecture VIII: Meetings on Prayer"

THE FAITH ENTERPRISE takes personal initiative. However, it is not primarily a self-initiative. Spiritual growth and life happen best in community. The Christian life is more of a pilgrimage than journey. One can set off alone on a journey, but pilgrimage, in its very nature, is meant to be done in group. Likewise, the Christian walk is a group activity, more like a team sport than an individual sport.

We are exhorted to find life together in the many "one another" descriptions in the Bible. Love one another. Bear with one another. Forgive one another. Share with one another. And so on. Jesus assumed that we would pray with one another.

Prayer seems to push community to a higher level. Jesus promised his unique manifest presence when we are in community prayer

> *Again, I say to you, if two of you agree on earth about anything they ask, it will be done for them by my Father in heaven. For where two or three are gathered in my name, there am I among them.[3]*

Since he said that he would be with us to the end of the age,[4] there has to be some unique and special sense of his presence when we are gathered in his name and in prayer.

This sense of Christ's presence in the community played out in the launching of the early church. In Acts 1, Jesus gave his followers his final instructions. They were to wait for the

---

3   Matthew 18:19–20

4   Matthew 28:18–20

promise of the Holy Spirit who would give them power in witness. So, when Jesus ascended into heaven, the followers went to the upper room where they were in one accord, "devoting themselves to prayer."[5]

It should not escape our attention that Luke's first description of the life of the early followers of Jesus after his ascension is a prayer meeting.[6] Even in its brief description we can see it was an intense and unified prayer gathering.

The next manifestation of Jesus was the release of the Spirit of Jesus on the gathered believers. There were bold demonstrations of his presence—a sound like wind, tongues of fire, spoken tongues, interpreting ears, and most importantly, bold announcement of good news that led to many people being restored in relationship to their Creator.

All of this was precipitated in prayer. Community prayer. United prayer. Devoted prayer.

Waiting on God in the upper room and the experience of Pentecost were so powerful to the church that its early history involved daily prayer. They devoted themselves to apostolic training, fellowship, the Lord's table, and the prayers.[7] Notice the use of the definite articles "the prayers" and not more generally "prayers." The early church relied on daily, planned times of meeting, to seek God's face together.

The manifestations of Christ's presence in their midst is seen in that early gathered community. They experienced...

---

5   Acts 1:14

6   Acts 1:14

7   Acts 2:42–47

...awe

...signs and wonders

...sacrificial generosity

...glad hearts

...favor with outsiders

...the Lord adding to their number daily (Acts 2:43–47)

...healing (Acts 3)

...boldness of witness (Acts 4)

...many signs and wonders (Acts 5)

...growing ministry and increase of the word of God (Acts 6)

...vision to reach the Gentiles and laying down of racism/ethnocentrism (Acts 10)

...miraculous release from prison (Acts 12)

...and a mission plan to reach the world (Acts 13).

All of this was not the result of their own initiative. It was not the result of their own cleverness. They were united in prayer at each stage, and God released fruitfulness in response. The manifest presence of God accomplished what they could not, even with their best efforts.

Acts 4:23–31 is a powerful expression of this united prayer. Earlier in the chapter, Peter and John are imprisoned and then tried by the religious leaders for praying for the healing of the lame man in the name of Jesus. Once they were released, they returned to the church to give a report. Immediately, the believers went to united prayer: *"And when they heard it, they lifted their voices together to God..."*[8] The content of their prayer is revealing. It was filled with the Word. It acknowledged the

---

8   Acts 4:24

Sovereignty of God in history, expressly in culminating in the work of Christ, the Anointed One. It was not filled with fear and self-preservation. Their prayer was for boldness in their own witness in the face of opposition and a release of the Spirit's arm with accompanying healings, signs, and wonders.

My experience has been that something unique happens in corporate prayer—prayer in community—that takes me beyond my own personal practice of prayer. I set aside time each morning to maintain the solace and separation needed to foster an ear of dialogue with God. I take the Spirit's admission through Paul to "pray without ceasing"[9] or to "pray at all times in the Spirit"[10] seriously. However, I would be half the man in Christ that I am today without regular, devoted, and communal prayer.

I have been in active discipleship and leading the church through the vocation of ministry for nearly thirty-five years. During every epoch of that pilgrimage, I have had a group of people whom I met with weekly to intercede in prayer. During different periods of the pilgrimage, I have participated in two, three, four, even five groups that met regularly to wait on the Lord. It is only in this most recent period of itinerant global ministry that I do not have that regular community. I am suddenly aware of a missing aspect of my pilgrimage—community-gathered, regularly devoted, agreeing prayer.

Why? Because the Holy Spirit speaks profoundly through the various vantage points of the group that inspires me or

9   I Thessalonians 5:17

10   Ephesians 6:18

illumines me in ways that I might have missed on my own. And Jesus said that something unique would happen—his manifest presence—when we agree together in prayer.

One of my favorite experiences of this type of movement I refer to as "Nathan on the cross." In Chapter 10, I talked about the notion of waiting on God and told the story of the years-long search for a pastor at our church. During this time, we had a weekly prayer gathering to seek God's guidance. During one of those prayer times, deep into the search, one of our prophetic pray-ers saw the name of the next associate pastor to be hired on the cross at the front of the sanctuary. I had prayed this simple prayer as we began our prayer time: "Maybe, Lord, you will even reveal a name to us." Immediately she saw in the Spirit the name "Nathan" etched across the cross.

Later that evening or the next morning, she e-mailed the name to me. At that point in the search process, we had reviewed eight resumes but none of the candidates had the name "Nathan." One of the previous Senior Pastors was named Nate, so I wondered if it was a word to find someone of the same quality of life and leadership as that pastor. Without clarity, I forgot about the prophetic vision as we continued the hard work of praying, interviewing, and discerning.

Our hard work over the next months brought us to a candidate that would be presented to the congregation. When we made the announcement to the congregation regarding the pastoral candidate, we included his name, bio, and resume, with details surrounding the ongoing search process.

We were presenting Nathan Hart to the congregation for the role of Associate Pastor.

When the pray-er who saw the vision on the cross received

the information, she re-sent me the e-mail that she had sent months earlier. I had completely forgotten that the name that she had seen on the cross was "Nathan."

The day before I met Nathan to begin the formal interview process, one of our other pray-ers heard God say to stop praying for the items on her personal prayer list and listen. God proceeded to describe the new pastor to her. She sent me an e-mail with around ten descriptors of the new pastor, including how he parted his hair. When I met Nathan the next day, he was everything that the Lord had revealed to her in advance. I joked with the pray-er later that she could have closed the deal with a Social Security number.

Even with this strong prophetic image, I still followed the rigorous due diligence of a healthy search process. I kept the prophetic words until the appropriate time, until the prophetic could be confirmation of God's leading and not a factor driving the church's decision. It was great fun the night when Nathan was confirmed as new associate pastor by a congregational vote to give these prophetic words and images to the body of Christ after the fact.

Those mysterious revelations were the glorious moments of prayer. And now looking back, we can say with great praise, "Look what God did!" However, the two years before we called this pastor, the congregation was frustrated with leadership because we weren't moving fast enough in calling a pastor. Over that period, there were a number of good candidates who would have worked fine, but they were not the candidates for us, only because they were not the ones that God had chosen. There was nothing wrong with each candidate except that they were not the ones selected by God.

And if we needed more from the Lord, Nathan was later called by the Lord and confirmed by the congregation as Senior Pastor when I moved to itinerant ministry. Agreement prayer: agreeing together, with God, for his design in our lives and for our world.

PRACTICAL EXERCISES

Find a group of people that you can pray with regularly. And pray. You may have to be the initiator. It is worth the effort.

I live in a very engaged and active community. I found that the only way I could gather people together was to set aside time in the early morning. I recommend this practice to you.

At our church, we had a group of three to four mothers with little children at home who wanted such a group. Their schedules made it impossible to be physically together. Thus, they decided to meet one day per week via Google Hangout. Seeing each other made it more of a connection. The only time they could do this was early in the morning before family responsibilities took over. Thus they had a rule: come as you are! No make-up externally, no posturing internally. With first cup of coffee in hand, cobwebs slowly disappearing, they became a community like that in Acts 1, waiting together on the Lord.

30

PRAYER AND WORD

The richness of God's Word ought to determine our prayer, not the poverty of our heart.

—DIETRICH BONHOEFFER[1]

The Book of Psalms is the Bible's hymnbook. It will show you what it means to walk with God in prayer and praise.

—BILLY GRAHAM[2]

PRAYER IS WARFARE. Along with feet fitted with the gospel and the Word of God, prayer is the most offensive part of our spiritual armor. The breastplate of righteousness, the helmet of salvation, and the shield of faith are defensive. The belt of truth holds everything together. But the sword of the Spirit—the Word—prayed and taken into our broken world is a proactive attack on darkness.

---

1   Bonhoeffer, *The Bonhoeffer Reader*, p. 564

2   Graham, *Billy Graham in Quotes*, p. 39

To be effective, prayer must be in alignment with the will of God,[3] and our clearest understanding of his will is found in the Word of God. Given those two realities—warfare and will—I find it very reassuring to simply pray the Word of God.

We actually see the principle of praying the Word of God in the early church. In Acts 4, the gathered believers pray for boldness in the face of early opposition against the church. A good portion of their recorded prayer is a quote of Psalm 2.[4] Eckhard Schnabel writes about the reflex of the early church to pray Scripture:

> The believers pray with the words of the Spirit as they pray with the words of Scripture, which God has spoken through the Spirit. Living in an age where many value originality and creativity above anything else, the prayer in vv. 24–30 teaches us that we are well advised if we use the words of Scripture in our prayers.[5]

In spiritual warfare, Jesus had the natural reflex to go to the Word of God to counter the temptations of Satan. On the cross, three of Jesus' seven final recorded phrases are prayers. One is simply a recitation of Psalm 22.

I learned to pray the Word from my prayer mentor, Carl Tonnessen, to whom I dedicated this book. Carl would pray the Word of God back to God. *God you said ... so I am asking for*

---

3   I John 5:14

4   Acts 4:23–31

5   Schnabel, *Acts*, loc. 7329–7330 [kindle]

that to be done for so-and-so. God in your Word it says ... release it in our day.

I have been giving you examples of praying the Word throughout the book. The book itself has almost 300 biblical references. Why? Because I have lived a life saturated in God's Word. That Word sustains me, directs me, challenges me, encourages me, convicts me, and gives me a God perspective on my world. It only makes sense to embed the Word into my prayer life.

Word and prayer are the two most fundamental lifelines to a vibrant spiritual life.

Prayer is my active dialogue with God, at the core of which I am telling him how I want my world to line up to his vision for the world. I am closest to that vision in his written Word.

To grow into this practice, it may be good to simply recite some of the prayers recorded in the Bible. The Psalms are prayers. There are many prayers of our God-pursuing ancestors that are recorded in the Word. We would do well to simply pray these prayers.

Join Abraham in his pleading for a wayward people.[6] Plagiarize Moses in praying for healing for those that we love.[7] Mimic Nehemiah in praying for success.[8] Follow Jesus in praying for unity among the people of God.[9] Use their actual prayers. Personalize the prayers by inserting contemporary situations.

---

6   Genesis 18

7   Numbers 12

8   Numbers 1

9   John 17

Another good source of praying the Word is following the manner in which the Apostle Paul described his prayer for the church. Consider the following two examples of his prayer for the church at Ephesus.

For this reason, because I have heard of your faith in the Lord Jesus and your love toward all the saints, I do not cease to give thanks for you, remembering you in my prayers, that the God of our Lord Jesus Christ, the Father of glory, may give you the Spirit of wisdom and of revelation in the knowledge of him, having the eyes of your hearts enlightened, that you may know what is the hope to which he has called you, what are the riches of his glorious inheritance in the saints, and what is the immeasurable greatness of his power toward us who believe, according to the working of his great might that he worked in Christ when he raised him from the dead and seated him at his right hand in the heavenly places, far above all rule and authority and power and dominion, and above every name that is named, not only in this age but also in the one to come.[10]

Paul shows the depths of his prayer. He begins with thanksgiving for what God was already doing in the life of the church body—faith and love were flowing. Then Paul reveals some of his intercession points: 1) Holy Spirit wisdom and revelation; 2) spiritual eyes of heart open; 3) experiential knowledge of hope and inheritance; 4) realization of power.

His second prayer report later in the letter is similar.

---

10   Ephesians 1:15–21

For this reason I bow my knees before the Father, from whom every family in heaven and on earth is named, that according to the riches of his glory he may grant you to be strengthened with power through his Spirit in your inner being, so that Christ may dwell in your hearts through faith—that you, being rooted and grounded in love, may have strength to comprehend with all the saints what is the breadth and length and height and depth, and to know the love of Christ that surpasses knowledge, that you may be filled with all the fullness of God.

Now to him who is able to do far more abundantly than all that we ask or think, according to the power at work within us, to him be glory in the church and in Christ Jesus throughout all generations, forever and ever. Amen.[11]

Paul begins by showing the intensity of his prayer. He bows the knee—an expression of humble plea. In this prayer, he again asks for strength, power, and experiential knowledge of God's bounty directed toward the people. Finally, he breaks forth into doxology—spontaneous praise. The content of his praise reveals the expectation that he placed in God's response to prayer. More than we could ask or think (or imagine)!

We have prayed these exact prayers from the letter to the Ephesians over people multiple times. It is fun to watch their shoulders go back and their countenance lifted up even as the Word is prayed over them. We do not have to wait for someone to pray over us. We can pray through God's Word for ourselves.

---

11   Ephesians 3:14–21

J. Oswald Sanders noted how his life and spiritual pursuit in prayer were transformed by praying God's Word. "A change came when I learned to use the Scriptures as a prayer book, and to turn what I read, especially in the Psalms, into prayer."[12]

In some ways, praying the Word is like seeding it into our lives. And the prophet Isaiah reminds us,

> *For as the rain and the snow come down from heaven*
> *   and do not return there but water the earth,*
> *making it bring forth and sprout,*
> *   giving seed to the sower and bread to the eater,*
> *so shall my word be that goes out from my mouth;*
> *   it shall not return to me empty,*
> *but it shall accomplish that which I purpose,*
> *   and shall succeed in the thing for which I sent it.*[13]

Praying the Word is agreeing with God's declared will and desires over our lives. His desires as described in the Word are flourishing, fruitfulness, and favor.

The writer of the letter to the Hebrews describes God's Word as living and active, reaching into the very core of our being:

> *For the word of God is living and active, sharper than any*
> *two-edged sword, piercing to the division of soul and of spirit,*
> *of joints and of marrow, and discerning the thoughts and inten-*
> *tions of the heart.*[14]

---

12   Duewel. "How to Use God's Word for a Vibrant Prayer Life"

13   Isaiah 55:10–11

14   Hebrews 4:12

If I am left to my own thoughts, my prayers will remain insipid. Praying the Word has the ability to bring transformation to my life.

PRACTICAL EXERCISES

Prayer and Bible reading go hand-in-hand. What is your present plan in systematically reading God's Word?

If you do not have a plan, why not consider reading a Psalm a day and connecting it to your prayer life?

I recommend reading every fifth Psalm to avoid getting into one theme day after day. There are 150 Psalms, so this could be done as a one-month experiment. Read the Psalm quietly. Reflect on the content of the Psalm.

What does it say about God?

What does it say about you as a human in search of God?

What does it say about our world?

Once you have explored the content of the Psalm, pray it out loud, inserting personal pronouns to make it more personal. A final exercise might be to write your own version of a prayer that follows the themes of the Psalm. Then, pray that prayer out loud as well.

31

PRAYER AND EMBODIMENT

It never occurred to me that Paul's "pray without ceasing" might actually be possible. It never occurred to me that praying could include thinking, that praying could be done with my eyes open, that praying could be done standing, sitting, driving, dancing, skiing, lying down, jogging, working.

—MICHAEL YACONELLI[1]

I cross myself because this gesture expresses my faithfulness to the will of God, admission of my personal sinfulness and my desire to be set free from it.

—LEO TOLSTOY, DIARY, 1908[2]

DEPENDING ON YOUR CHRISTIAN TRADITION and your religious experiences, you have certain attitudes and feelings about ritualized form. I grew up in middle America, in a Protestant holiness

---

1   Yaconelli, *Messy Spirituality*, p.10

2   Romanov, "Tolstoy and the Sign of the Cross"

movement. At the time I did not realize it, but today I would describe it as a flat social structure. We had a religious assumption that faith was to be expressed spontaneously. As a result, we were suspicious of ritual in worship, especially the rituals of others that were different than our own experience. I find this interesting as all church traditions have ritual.

I have come to embrace the importance of the embodiment of our faith practice. What I do with my body can significantly reinforce or even redirect the intentions of my heart.

One of our prayer rituals growing up was to kneel in prayer. It was common for us to kneel in front of metal chairs in a circle in the basement of the church for prayer meeting on Wednesday night. There were times of special prayer where we knelt in the pews of the church as we interceded for a kingdom-of-God intervention.

If we were sitting during prayer it was assumed that our heads would be bowed, our eyes closed, and even our hands folded. These were physical expressions of humility. And the closing of eyes was to take away any distractions. In fact, it was almost implied that it would be rebellious to pray with eyes open.

There are many examples of kneeling in prayer in the Bible,[3] and I am sure these multiple examples informed our preference for kneeling. Daniel knelt three times per day in the direction of Jerusalem to pray.[4] Paul described a moment of intensity in his own prayer life where he knelt before the

---

3   1Kings 8:54; II Chronicles 6:1; Psalm 95:6; Acts 9:40, 20:36

4   Daniel 3:10

Father.[5] Church tradition recounts that James had knees like a camel because he spent so much time in that prayer position.

Tertullian, an early church father (A.D. 155–240), noted that early Christians used multiple prayer positions, but they preferred standing in prayer. They were following another common practice of God's people in Scripture. It was common to pray with eyes open and looking toward heaven.

When Jesus prayed at the resurrection of Lazarus he was standing, and he lifted up his eyes.[6] (However, he knelt in the garden to pray before his crucifixion.[7])

And rather than folding hands in prayer, the more common form in the Bible was with open or raised hands toward heaven in an expression of reception. Paul stated that he preferred men to pray with lifted holy hands in his letter to Timothy.[8]

Abraham fell on his face before God in prayer.[9] Moses prayed with outstretched arms before God.[10] Nehemiah prayed simultaneously while engaging the king in a serious conversation.[11] Jonah prayed prone in the belly of the great fish and under the shade of a great plant.[12]

---

5   Ephesians 3:14

6   John 11:41

7   Luke 22:41

8   I Timothy 2:8

9   Genesis 17:3,17

10   Exodus 9:27–29

11   Nehemiah 2:4

12   Jonah 2:1–9; 4:6ff

We can easily exalt one posture over another. However, much like with fasting, the posture of the heart is more important in prayer than the posture of our bodies. Nevertheless, the position of our bodies can lead the way to correctly position our hearts in prayer.

With that understanding, I suggest that you develop a posture that helps you enter into the right attitude in prayer. Sometimes the urgency of my prayer concern makes kneeling helpful. In corporate intercession, I like to turn my hands up toward heaven in a position of receiving. Other times I will find myself rocking as I wait on the Lord. And the majority of the time, I now pray with my eyes open. I have learned to listen to and watch God's movements around me in nature, in the people that I am praying with, and in the atmosphere.

I also think it is wise to vocalize our prayer when we have a setting that will allow it. Praying in my mind can easily lead to distraction or rabbit trails in my thoughts. Praying out loud has a way of reinforcing the dialogue nature of my prayer.

Another form of embodied prayer for me is writing my prayers out. I have described this process at times as if my hand has its own mind and just takes off. I know that is not physiologically correct, but still, I will come to the end of a few sentences of prayer that I am writing to the Lord and wonder how I arrived there.

It is also interesting how often, immediately after writing the prayer, there will be a response or affirmation in the portion of the Word of God that I am reading for the day. It feels like spontaneous exchange, but the Spirit has been directing the conversation. An added benefit of writing prayers is eliminating the second-guessing of whether I am hearing from the Lord or not. I can dismiss a thought as my own fabrication, but a written word takes on more certainty.

Sometimes the prayer pump can be primed by praying out loud with the prayers of saints that have gone before us. I pray the Lorica of St. Patrick over myself, my family, and my places of influence every morning (see Appendix 3). I have prayed other historical prayers at different points of my life. Right now, I am praying the following prayer of Blaise Pascal (1623–1662) every day as my declaration before the Lord.

> Lord, let me not henceforth desire life or health,
> except to expend them for you, with you, and in you.
> You alone know what is good for me,
> do therefore what seems best to you.
> Give to me or take from me,
> conform my will to yours,
> and grant that with humble and perfect submission,
> and with holy confidence,
> I might receive the orders of your eternal providence,
> and might mutually receive all that comes to me, from you,
> through Jesus Christ our Lord.

I have memorized both the Lorica and this prayer so that I can pray them directly to the Lord in the flow of our conversation.

It doesn't matter what posture you take; the key is to put yourself in a holy space, holy position, and holy attitude to approach the throne of grace.

What posture makes you feel most attuned to God for prayer?

Experiment with different ritual forms. Stick with new forms for a while until they become more familiar and natural.

There are a number of historical prayers in Appendix 3. I recommend that you find one that resonates with your present reality and pray it out loud as a way of launching into personal, more spontaneous prayer. You can also go back over each line and personalize the prayer.

32

PRAYER IN THE NAME OF JESUS

Pray, always pray; when sickness wastes thy frame, prayer brings the healing power of Jesus' name.

—A.B. SIMPSON

Prayer is the one prime, eternal condition by which the Father is pledged to put the Son in possession of the world. Christ prays through His people. Had there been importunate, universal, and continuous prayer by God's people, long ere this the earth had been possessed for Christ.

—E.M. BOUNDS[1]

I GREW UP WITH A SIMPLE FORMAT TO PRAYER. We were taught to address God as Father. This was clearly a close following of the Lord's Prayer. We did not recite the Lord's Prayer in our praise-worship gatherings. We memorized it but rarely recited it.

We weren't forbidden from addressing God in prayer with

---

1   Bounds, "God Shapes the World through Prayer"

other designations such as Lord or God. But praying to our Heavenly Father was our preferred pattern. This seemed to be Jesus' preferred pattern on the cross so it cannot be too far off:

Father, forgive them.[2]

Father, into your hands I commit my spirit![3]

We always closed our prayers with the words "In Jesus' name. Amen," or "in the name of Jesus. Amen." It was so engrained into my practice as child that when someone closes prayer without mentioning the name of Jesus, it feels like something is missing. I believe that this practice was also followed in observation of one of Jesus' teachings on prayer.

Toward the end of his ministry on earth, Jesus challenged his disciples that until that point, "they had not asked for anything in his name."[4] This was immediately preceded by his invitation to ask anything "in his name." He actually repeated this invitation three different times.[5] He was inviting them and us to a new authority in our prayer life.[6]

In that teaching, I do not believe that Jesus was calling them to a slavish literalism. To pray in his name was to pray out of the relationship established in his name. The Scriptures remind us of the uniqueness of the name of Jesus.

---

2   Luke 23:34

3   Luke 23:46

4   John 16:24

5   John 14:13–14; 15:16; 16:23

6   John 16:26

Christ Jesus is the "name above all names."[7]

Salvation is found in no other name."[8]

Repentance, forgiveness of sins, and spiritual life come from his name.[9]

As a result, when the disciples continued the ministry of Jesus after his ascension, they saw their fruitfulness as flowing from their relationship with God through the name of Jesus.

In Acts 3, God uses Peter and John to bring healing to a man paralyzed from birth who was sitting outside the Temple. Peter announced the healing in the name of Jesus. He explained the healing to the onlookers as being the result of the name of Jesus, and particularly faith in the name of Jesus.

In Acts 4, the religious leaders asked Peter and John by what name or authority did they heal the man. The leaders of the day had an assumption that such power was only possible in the name of God or the name of Satan. This is why, earlier, these same leaders accused Jesus as working in the power of Beelzebub.[10] Peter once again pointed to the uniqueness and power of the name of Jesus.

Peter mentioned the phrase "in the name of Jesus" five

---

7   Philippians 2:9–11

8   Acts 4:12

9   Luke 24:47; Acts 10:43; John 20:31; I John 2:12

10   Luke 11:14–23

times over two chapters, as well as "through Jesus" to point to the authority source for the miracle. The implications were unmistakable to the religious leaders who then responded to Peter and John by forbidding them to *teach or speak at all in the name of Jesus.*[11]

Understanding the culture of that period in time might help us understand this notion of praying in Jesus' name.

The American conception of a name is that it is a way of referring to something or someone. However, the biblical conception of a name was that it was a description of essence. The practice of changing one's name to mark a change in character reflects this understanding:

> In the biblical thought a name is not a mere label of identification; it is an expression of the essential nature of its bearer. A man's name reveals his character. … hence to know the name of God is to know God as he revealed himself (Ps. 9:10).[12]

To know God's name experientially is a suggestion of relationship. It is also a sign of entering under the blessing of his attributes and protection.

Jesus told his disciples that they would demonstrate the kingdom in his name. He sent them out to do the same things that he did. Jesus announced the kingdom, healed the sick, and cast out demons. We see these three activities repeated by his followers in Luke 9 and 10. When the Twelve went out, they

---

11   Acts 4:18

12   Buttrick, *The Interpreter's Dictionary of the Bible*, Vol. 3, p. 500–501

proclaimed the kingdom, healed the sick, and cast out demons. When the Seventy-Two returned from their itinerant kingdom ministry, they reported to Jesus that *"Even the demons submit to us in your name."*[13]

This relationally based privilege and responsibility was so clear to the early followers of Jesus that their corporate prayer was summarized with these words:

Stretch out your hand to heal and perform miraculous signs and wonders through the name of your holy servant Jesus.[14]

To pray in the name of Jesus was to point to an intimate relationship to Jesus and obedience to his desired outcomes for any situation in our world.

The significance of the name of Jesus in relation to prayer deserves special notice. To pray in the name of Jesus, to ask anything in His name... is not merely to add to one's prayers a meaningless formula, but it is to ask something from God as Christ's representative on earth, in His missions and stead, in His spirit, and in His aim. Such a phrase correctly understood, cannot help but govern the kind and quality of the prayers Christians pray.[15]

---

13   Luke 10:17

14   Acts 4:30

15   *The International Standard Bible Encyclopedia*, Vol. 3, p. 483

SPEAK UP! LISTEN UP!

This is not a formula or a magic incantation to be automatically and unthinkingly appended to every prayer; it is a demonstration of our willingness to be united with the will of the Lord Jesus. We should ask ourselves, *Does this request really blend with the lifestyle, the desires, the spirit, and the attitude of Jesus Christ? Would Jesus pray this way to the Father?* Having passed such a test, we then can have great boldness and assurance as we speak with the Father.[16]

The question always comes up: can't this tag line become meaningless or even a form of magical incantation over time? Absolutely. We have the example in Scripture of the sons of Sceva who tried to use Jesus' name as a magical formula without the underlying relationship with Jesus. This turned out miserably for them.[17] Likewise, Jesus warned of the danger of using his name without really knowing him in relationship.[18]

I do not want to discourage the practice of using Jesus' name because of potential danger. Nor do I want to suggest that a prayer is incomplete when the words "in Jesus' name" are not used to close the prayer. If a person is praying out of the understanding of their union with Christ, words are not necessary to validate the prayer. Extremes on either side are silly.

All the same, with a proper understanding of the real significance of praying in Jesus' name, I still highly recommend vocalizing that we are praying in Jesus' name. Why? The spirit

16   Comfort and Hawley, *Opening John's Gospel and Epistles*, p. 206

17   Acts 18

18   Matthew 7:22

world is listening in on our prayer life. God hears our thoughts, but the spirit world is not omniscient and always able to hear our thoughts. Establishing the authority bounds of our prayer can change the spiritual atmosphere.

There is power in the name of Jesus.

PRACTICAL EXERCISES

Have you thought about the reality of praying in Jesus' name in the past?

If it is not your practice, consider praying in Jesus' name for a week to orient yourself to the practice.

33

DESPERATION

We will never have pure enough motives, or be good enough, or know enough in order to pray rightly. We simply must set all these things aside and begin praying.

—RICHARD FOSTER[1]

Prayer does not "work" because it somehow allows us to harness divine favor. Rather, prayer is the opportunity to tell the truth about our need for God. Similarly, the other Christian disciplines do not elevate us to a higher plane of living as the true people of God. At best, they are all acts of confession. … a way of confessing our inability ever to get it right, and that without the grace of God in Jesus Christ we would have no hope of leading meaningful lives.

—M. CRAIG BARNES[2]

---

1   Foster, *Prayer*, p. 8

2   Barnes, *Yearning*, p. 62

I HAVE HAD THE PRIVILEGE OF SERVING in one of the poorest areas of the world. Mali was listed as the sixth poorest nation in the world by the United Nations when we lived there. I have also had the privilege of serving in a city in Connecticut that at that time was the wealthiest city in the world with more than 50,000 inhabitant. There were ZIP codes with a higher income per capita but not with that large of a population.

Physical poverty is obvious and naturally drives us to prayer.

Spiritual poverty is less obvious, especially when it is hidden with material wealth.

Sadly, financial or physical blessing can demotivate us to pray.

One of my prayers when I first arrived in this city was "Lord, could we come to know the poverty of our hearts without experiencing financial poverty. Would you revive us without destroying us?" That might sound odd to some. But as a parent might inflict discomfort on a child for their long-term good, God in his love might impact our material comfort to give us something better.

My experience is that most people are not driven to a deeper relationship with God when all goes well. Usually, people only get serious about pursuing God in prayer when trouble visits their lives. Physical sickness has a way of undercutting our confidence in wealth, as does a broken relationship, a lost job, or a wandering child.

Sadly, sometimes when those places of deprivation have been restored, I have watched people once again lose their passion to pursue God.

Decline in prayer is an outward sign of spiritual poverty. Churches in the affluent West have minimized prayer. It receives a small portion of time in our gathered worship-praise services. Interestingly, the early Christians followed a synagogue model of gathering where nearly a third of the gathering was given to prayer.

We tend to seek out programs, events, or practical solutions to address spiritual problems. We are rarely driven to the desperation of waiting on God for his kingdom to come. It doesn't appear that the early church was programmatic. They followed principles, but they seemed more often to wait on God in prayer.

Our movement away from prayer has not been intentional. It was a slow drift. The reflections of Schnabel are insightful on the process of losing our passion or perceived sense of need for God.

> In the hectic pace of life in modern societies, while it may not lead to a denial of the value of prayer, it easily leads to minimization of time reserved for prayer. As a result, people who profess to be Christians may pray rarely and only in 'organized' situations in church.[3]

Given how little time is given to corporate prayer in the contemporary church, this is concerning.

When I began as a pastor in New Jersey, we served a mixed socio-economic community. The congregation on average was lower-middle class. Our church body never grew consistently beyond 200 worshippers on a Sunday. However, we consistently had 30–60 in attendance for Wednesday night prayer.

When we served the church in Mali, we could easily get

---

3   Schnabel, *Acts*, loc. 7314 [kindle]

30–60 from a similar size church to pray all night. The average Malian lived on $300 per year. They were more desperate for God's daily provision.

When serving in Greenwich, I beat the drum of prayer over and over. I initiated a fresh emphasis twice a year for nine years. I provided prayer cards to go along with sermon series. I could not seem to mobilize more than 6–8 people regularly and consistently to gather for the simple act of prayer. And that church was three times the size of the church that I pastored in New Jersey. We were too wealthy and busy to add corporate prayer.

Interestingly, there was a correlation between the breadth of united prayer and the miracles and divine interventions that we experienced in each of those places as well.

Affluence demotivates prayer. I write this not in judgment but as observation. My comments are descriptive of my experience and not meant to be a solid rule.

When we observe a person who has a lot of material gain, we have this reflex to think "wow, are they blessed!" It is not surprising. Even the ancient Hebrew worldview assumed that external wealth was a sign of God's favor. But being blessed has little to do with what we have but where we find our confidence.

So, we might be better off to say that a person has a better chance of being blessed if they are physically and materially in a state of deprivation. Physical well-being and material gain may be a hindrance to being really blessed. This is what Jesus had in mind when he referred to how hard it is for a rich person to enter the kingdom of God.[4]

Desperation is a friend of prayer.

---

4   Matthew 19:23

O Lord, keep my heart desperate for you, knowing its poverty state without you!

An interesting account in the Old Testament illustrates this principle.[5] Naaman was a commander in the army of the king of Syria. Not only did he have influence, he was described as a man of valor. We learn in his story that he was quite wealthy—at least materially.

But he was a leper. Leprosy was living death. So, he was desperate.

Through a series of divinely orchestrated events, he approached the prophet Elisha to seek healing. He arrived with his horses and chariots—a statement of power. The prophet sent his servant to Naaman to give him instructions to be healed.

Go and wash in the Jordan seven times, and your flesh will be restored, and you shall be clean.[6]

Naaman was angry and went away in a rage.

Naaman's pride was in the way of his healing. He did not get the reception from the prophet that he felt he deserved as a man of influence and means. The prophet did only addressed him through his servant and not in person. And it did not make sense, nor was it proper, to be sent away to the dirty waters of the Jordan. He wanted the prophet to simply declare healing over him.

As he was leaving, his servants came near to him to speak wisdom. Naaman was desperate, so he laid his pride down

---

5   II Kings 5:1–14

6   II Kings 5:10

and went to the Jordan River to follow the instructions of the prophet. He was healed on the spot. He went from a proud man to a man who worshipped the living God of Israel.

Desperation is a friend of prayer.

So, what does one do if they are physically and financially affluent? Holy desperation can be the byproduct of two realities. First, coming to realize our spiritual poverty can move us away from a sense of confidence in our wealth. Second, finding a holy discontent can help us direct our prayer and wealth toward the brokenness of our world. A holy discontent is a sense of righteous anger about some aspect of the impact of sin that has broken our world. I have friends whose passion is directed toward issues and areas of desperation in our world—accessible drinking water or medical supplies, modern slavery through sex trafficking, accessibility to quality education, lack of contact with a viable witness of the Good News, to name a few. These places of desperation have become motivators toward prayer and service.

We can remain desperate even in our plenty. May God help us all.

PRACTICAL EXERCISES

What is your DQ, Desperation Quotient? How desperate are you for God? Where has comfort or material blessing weakened your sense of urgency in prayer?

What can you do to increase your DQ?

When has your DQ been the highest in your life? Can you get back to that level of need without experiencing the same physical or material deprivations?

Ask God to awaken your own sense of spiritual poverty without Christ.

34

THE GREAT EXCHANGE

We make a private chapel of our heart where we can retire from time to time to commune with Him, peacefully, humbly, lovingly.

—BR. LAWRENCE[1]

Learning to pray doesn't offer us a less busy life; it offers us a less busy heart.

—PAUL MILLER[2]

TO BE HEARD BY GOD and to hear from God are reward enough in prayer. And there are many more promises and benefits related to prayer. One is peace.

There are many realities that strike at our sense of well-being in our contemporary, fast-paced, social-media-saturated lives. One result is that I observe anxiety as an epidemic that is paralyzing many people. God offers us shalom. The world

---

1   Lawrence, *The Practice of the Presence of God*, p. 65

2   Miller, *A Praying Life*, p. 11

overwhelms us with noise. We actually need to proactively resist that interruption and confusion.

The apostle Paul, under the inspiration of the Holy Spirit, offers a solution in his letter to the church in Philippi. I call it the great exchange—my anxiety for his peace.

Rejoice in the Lord always; again I will say, rejoice. Let your reasonableness be known to everyone. The Lord is at hand; do not be anxious about anything, but in everything by prayer and supplication with thanksgiving let your requests be made known to God. And the peace of God, which surpasses all understanding, will guard your hearts and your minds in Christ Jesus.[3]

Paul begins with rejoicing. The letter could be called the letter of joy. Paul writes from prison, but his message is one of overwhelming joy in spite of his circumstances. We are not surprised, because when God used him in the establishment of the church in Philippi, he ended up in prison. Instead of grumbling in his circumstances, he was praising and singing at midnight when the kingdom of God came breaking in to the prison, leading to the salvation of the Philippian jailer's family.

So, prayer begins in praise, rejoicing. When we see God for **who he is** then our circumstances are reduced in size in comparison to his greatness. We then are not alone in our challenges that create anxiety: *"the Lord is at hand."*

Then the exchange—

"Do not be anxious about anything." Anything. Everything. Regardless of how menacing.

---

3   Philippians 4:4–7

"*But by prayer and supplication.*" Tell God.

"*And the peace of God, which surpasses all understanding, will guard your hearts and your minds in Christ Jesus.*" Unexplainable. Anxiety out there. Peace in here. My heart guarded in Christ Jesus.

If we look closely, we see another aspect of our prayer understanding: "*in Christ Jesus.*" Relationally secure, we pray in his name, in his finished work, in his security, and in his authority.

Now, sometimes the circumstances are so overwhelming or so menacing that we need to make the great exchange multiple times in a day, even within an hour. And it also means that we need to take on all the aspects of prayer: Praise, Thanksgiving, Word, Confession.

Paul has already situated prayer in Praise with his call to rejoice.

He has already noted that supplication travels hand-in-hand with Thanksgiving.

And the following verses link it to the Word.

Finally, brothers, whatever is true, whatever is honorable, whatever is just, whatever is pure, whatever is lovely, whatever is commendable, if there is any excellence, if there is anything worthy of praise, think about these things. What you have learned and received and heard and seen in me—practice these things, and the God of peace will be with you.[4]

The standard to measure all things true, honorable, just, pure, lovely, commendable, excellent, is the Word of God. By

---

4   Philippians 4:8–9

taking up the sword of the Spirit, we are promised another level of realization of the manifest presence of God: "*practice these things, and the God of peace will be with you.*"

God is at hand ... the God of peace will be with you.

Trading anxiety for peace—the great exchange.

I can illustrate from my own life. There was a time in Mali when I was struggling with an anxiety that had become a root of bitterness. My anxiety was related to a pastor who was very difficult to work with and who was blocking the work from going forward. He was simply a contrarian in the obnoxious sense of the word. If you said yes, he said no. And on the same issue, if you said no, he said yes.

I had developed resentment in my heart toward him. I was jogging one morning in conversation with the Lord. The Holy Spirit convicted me of my growing hatred toward this pastor. I would confess and repent. Then, within a couple minutes, this pastor would be back into my mind. I repeated the cycle several times. Anxiety was not being replaced with peace.

When I crested a bridge, I saw the African sun stretching across the distant horizon. It is not possible to explain in words the spectacle of the rising sun in flat areas of West Africa. It covers the whole horizon in oranges, pinks, and yellow tints or colors. Because of the desert dust you can look into it. That vision made me think of God in his creative majesty. And I began singing a praise song that we had been singing with the Malian believers.

> *Du lever du soleil jusqu'à son coucher,*
> *Bénissez l'Éternel Dieu, le Tout-Puissant!*
> *Du lever du soleil jusqu'à son coucher,*

Bénissez l'Éternel Dieu, le Tout-Puissant !

Bénissez Dieu, vous ses enfants, célébrez l'Éternel !
Béni soit le nom du Seigneur, dès maintenant et pour l'éternité!

The praise song is taken from Psalm 113:3: *From the rising of the sun to its setting, the name of the Lord is to be praised.*

I kept singing and singing, Word and praise together in prayer. Without realizing it, I forgot about the pastor who was in my head for the earlier part of my run and inner conversation. Word and praise saturated prayer left no room for anxiety or bitterness.

Oddly, that pastor changed in the weeks ahead. He no longer pushed me into anxiety.

Not really. I changed. Or better yet, God changed me. He was at hand. His peace overtook my anxiety.

35

ONE FINAL WORD FROM VENU

do not believe that one can earnestly seek and find the priceless treasure of God's call without a devout prayer life. That is where God speaks. The purpose of prayer and of God's call in your life is not to make you number one in the world's eyes, but to make him number one in your life. We must be willing to be outshone while shining for God. We hear very little about being smaller in our own self-estimate."

—RAVI ZACHARIAS[1]

I WAS SITTING AT MY COMPUTER ready to bring this book to closure. There is so much more to explore on this topic of prayer. I knew that there were to be thirty-five chapters, but I was uncertain what the final word would be. Another testimony from our lives? Another aspect of prayer?

As I was praying about closure, I decided to take my first peek at morning e-mail. A message had been sent to us from a friend in India. It was nighttime for him and daytime for us.

---

1   FaceBook post by Ravi Zacharias from March 15, 2015

Venu G to me, Ingrid
7:33 AM (2 hours ago)

Subject: **In case you need a reminder—"He Surely Hears YOU!"**

Dear Pastor Chuck and Ingrid,

"But God has surely listened and heard my voice in prayer. Praise be to God who has not rejected my prayer or withheld His love from me! Psa. 66: 19,20 ... My friend, be encouraged today, no prayer offered up to God is not heard and the psalmists says *"He listens."* That prayer you have been praying, that answer you have been waiting for, that miracle ...it just may happen this week. *"May God be gracious to us and bless us and make his face shine upon us ....THIS WEEK.* "Psa. 67:1. Blessings, victories, favor this week my friend. May He listen and hear your prayer, your request, your petition and mine too! Amen and Amen!

I cannot think of a better way to close this book

In case you need one more reminder: God hears you.

Speak up, he is listening. Listen up, he is speaking.

APPENDIX 1

THE LORICA OF ST. PATRICK

I arise today
Through a mighty strength, the invocation of the Trinity,
Through a belief in the Threeness,
Through confession of the Oneness
Of the Creator of creation.

I arise today
Through the strength of Christ's birth and his baptism,
Through the strength of his crucifixion and his burial,
Through the strength of his descent for the judgment of doom,
Through the strength of his resurrection and his ascension,
Through the strength of the expectation and hope of his immi-
nent return.

I arise today
Through the strength of the love of cherubim,
In obedience of angels,
In service of archangels,
In the hope of resurrection to meet with reward,
In the prayers of patriarchs,

In preachings of the apostles,
In faiths of confessors,
In innocence of virgins,
In deeds of righteous saints.

I arise today
Through God's strength to pilot me;
God's might to uphold me,
God's wisdom to guide me,
God's eye to look before me,
God's ear to hear me,
God's word to speak for me,
God's hand to guard me,
God's way to lie before me,
God's shield to protect me,
God's hosts to save me
From snares of the devil,
From temptations of vices,
From every one who desires me ill,
Afar and a near,
Alone or in a multitude.

I summon today all these powers between me and evil
Against every cruel merciless power that opposes my body and soul
Against all schemes and plans of the kingdom of darkness
Against all curses and false judgments spoken or unspoken
Against all accusations and lies of the enemy
Against all false agreements and unholy alliances conscious or
unconscious
Against every knowledge that corrupts man's body and soul

Christ shield me today!
Against any harm to my body, soul or spirit
Against any harm to my family, earthly or spiritual
Against any harm to the earthly things you have called me to
steward
So that I might live in the fullness of your blessing and abundance.

Christ with me, Christ before me, Christ behind me,
Christ in me, Christ beneath me, Christ above me,
Christ on my right, Christ on my left,
Christ when I lie down, Christ when I sit down, Christ when
I arise,
Christ in the heart of every one who thinks of me,
Christ in the mouth of every one who speaks of me,
Christ in the eye that sees me,
Christ in the ear that hears me.

As I move into this day, I appropriate all this for myself and for
all who are under my authority and influence.

I arise today
Through a mighty strength, the invocation of the Trinity,
Through a belief in the Threeness,
Through confession of the Oneness
Of the Creator of creation

ST. PATRICK (CIRCA 377)
CHANGES MADE BY CHUCK AND INGRID DAVIS, 2012

APPENDIX 2

THE NAMES OF GOD[1]

Day 1
God is **Jehovah**. The name of the independent, self-complete being—**"I AM WHO I AM"**—only belongs to Jehovah God. Our proper response to Him is to fall down in fear and awe of the One who possesses all authority.

−EXODUS 3:13-15

Day 2
God is **Jehovah-m'kaddesh**. This name means "the God who sanctifies." A God separate from all that is evil requires that the people who follow Him be cleansed from all evil.

−LEVITICUS 20:7,8

---

1   The list of names is adapted from https://www.navigators.org/resource/praying-names–attributes–god/. There are several books and websites that offer more resources regarding praying the names of God. Another good source is Appendix A from *Experiencing God*, by Henry Blackaby, LifeWay Press, 1990. He also includes names and descriptions of Jesus and the Holy Spirit to use in prayer.

Day 3

God is **Jehovah-jireh**. This name means "the God who provides." Just as He provided yesterday, He will also provide today and tomorrow. He grants deliverance from sin, the oil of joy for the ashes of sorrow, and eternal citizenship in His kingdom for all those adopted into His household.

–GENESIS 22:9-14

Day 4

God is Jehovah-shalom. This name means "the God of peace." We are meant to know the fullness of God's perfect peace, or His "shalom." God's peace surpasses understanding and sustains us even through difficult times. It is the product of fully being what we were created to be.

–JUDGES 6:16-24

Day 5

God is **Jehovah-rophe**. This name means "Jehovah heals." God alone provides the remedy for mankind's brokenness through His son, Jesus Christ. The Gospel is the physical, moral, and spiritual remedy for all people.

–EXODUS 15:22-26

Day 6
God is **Jehovah-nissi**. This name means "God our banner."
Under His banner we go from triumph to triumph and say,
"Thanks be to God, who gives us the victory through our Lord
Jesus Christ" (1 Corinthians 15:57).

—EXODUS 17:8-15

Day 7
God is **El-Shaddai**. This name means "God Almighty," the God
who is all-sufficient and all-bountiful, the source of all blessings.

—GENESIS 49:22-26

Day 8
God is **Adonai**. This name means "Master" or "Lord." God,
our Adonai, calls all God's people to acknowledge themselves
as His servants, claiming His right to reign as Lord of our lives.

—2 SAMUEL 7:18-20

APPENDIX 3

HISTORICAL PRAYERS

We beseech thee, Master, to be our helper and protector.
Save the afflicted among us; have mercy on the lowly;
raise up the fallen; appear to the needy; heal the ungodly;
restore the wanderers of thy people;
feed the hungry; ransom our prisoners;
raise up the sick; comfort the faint-hearted.

CLEMENT OF ROME, 1ST CENTURY

O Lord, who hast mercy upon all, take away from me my sins,
and mercifully kindle in me the fire of thy Holy Spirit.
Take away from me the heart of stone,
and give me a heart of flesh,
a heart to love and adore thee,
a heart to delight in thee,
to follow and to enjoy thee,
for Christ's sake. Amen

AMBROSE OF MILAN, CIRCA A.D. 339-97

Lord, for tomorrow and its needs, I do not pray;
Keep me, my God, from stain of sin just for today.
Let me both diligently work, and duly pray,
Let me be kind in word and deed, just for today.
Let me be slow to do my will, prompt to obey;
Help me to sacrifice myself, just for today.
And if today my tide of life should ebb away,
give me thy sacraments divine, sweet Lord, today.
So for tomorrow and its needs I do not pray,
but keep me, guide me, love me,
Lord, just for today.

AUGUSTINE, A.D. 354–430

Lord Jesus Christ, have mercy on me!
Lord Jesus Christ, Son of God,
have mercy on me, a sinner!

EGYPTIAN DESERT FATHERS, CIRCA A.D. 400

Lord,
I journey on my way.
What need I fear, when thou art near O king of night and day?
More safe am I within thy hand
than if a host did round me stand.
In Jesus, Amen.

COLUMBA, CIRCA A.D. 521–597

O God,
you have folded back
the mantle of the night
to clothe us in the golden glory of the day.

Drive from our hearts
all gloomy thoughts,
and make us glad
with the brightness of your hope,
that we may aspire
to heavenly virtues;
through Jesus Christ our Lord.

AN ANCIENT COLLECT, A. D. 590

Lord, hear my voice when I call to you.
My heart has prompted me to seek
your face; I seek it Lord; do not hide from me, alleluia. Guide me in your
truth and teach me, Lord, for you are the God who saves me. The path
I walk, Christ walks it.
May the land in which I am be without sorrow. May the Trinity protect
me wherever I stay, Father, Son and Holy Spirit. Amen

FROM THE KEEILLS *CELTIC PRAYER BOOK*

O Father, most merciful,
in the beginning you created us,
and by the passion of your only
Son you created us anew.
Work in us now,
both to will and to do what pleases you.
Since we are weak and can do no good
thing by ourselves,
grant us your grace and heavenly blessing,
that in whatever work we engage
we may do all to your honor and glory.
through the power of your Holy Spirit, Amen.

ANSELM, 11TH CENTURY

Guard us your children who, for love of your Name,
have made a pilgrimage to Celtic lands of blessing,
and return home to spread your blessing
to those who await our arrival.
May all of our life be conscious walking with you.
Be our companion on the way, our guide at the crossroads, our strength
in weariness,
our defense in dangers, our shelter on the path,
our shade in the heat, our light in darkness, our comfort in discourage-
ment, and the firmness of our intentions, that through your guidance we
may arrive
safely at the end of their journey and, enriched with grace and virtue, may
our return to our homes filled with salutary and lasting joy.

ADOPTED FROM THE "PILGRIM'S PRAYER,"
CODEX CALIXTINUS, 12TH CENTURY

O Lord,
grant that we may be numbered among those
chosen by God to be witnesses to your resurrection,
not only by word of mouth,
but in actions and truth,
for your honor and glory;
with the Father and the Holy Spirit
you live and reign as one God,
now and forever. Amen

LUDOLPH OF SAXONY, A.D. 1295–1378

God be with thee in every pass,
Jesus be with thee on every hill,
Spirit be with thee on every stream, headland and ridge and lawn;
Each sea and land, each
Moor and meadow,
Each lying down, each rising up,
In the trough of the waves,
On the crest of the billows,
Each step of the journey thou goest.

PRAYER OF THE SCOTTISH CROSS ("CARMINA GADELICA")

Strengthen me, O God,
by the grace of your Holy Spirit.
Strengthen my inner being,
and empty my heart of all useless care and anguish.
O Lord, grant me heavenly wisdom,
that I may learn to seek and to find you above all things,
to relish and to love you above all things,
and to think of all other things
as being at the disposal of your wisdom.

THOMAS À KEMPIS, A.D. 1380-1471

I thank you, my heavenly Father, through Jesus Christ, Your dear Son,
that You have kept me this night from all harm and danger; and I pray
that You, would keep me this day also from sin and every evil, that all
my doings and life may please you. For into your hands I commend myself,
my body and soul, and all things. Let your holy angels be with me, that
the evil foe may have no power over me. Amen.

"MORNING PRAYER," MARTIN LUTHER, A.D. 1483-1546

I thank you, my heavenly Father, through Jesus Christ, Your dear Son, that You have graciously kept me this day; and I pray that You would forgive me all my sins where I have done wrong, and graciously keep me this night. For into Your hands I commend myself, my body and soul, and all things. Let your holy angels be with me, that the evil foe may have no power over me. Amen

"EVENING PRAYER," MARTIN LUTHER, A.D. 1483-1546

Lord, teach me to be generous.
Teach me to serve you as you deserve;
to give and not to count the cost,
to fight and not to heed the wounds,
to toil and not to seek for rest,
to labor and not to ask for reward,
save that of knowing that I do your will.

IGNATIUS OF LOYOLA, A.D. 1491-1556

Christ, you have no physical body now on earth but ours, no hands but ours, no feet but ours. We are the eyes through which to look out your compassion to the world. We are the feet with which you are to go about doing good; We are the hands with which you bless humanity now. Make us, your body and the church, alert to your assignments today, to be your presence among those needing a touch from you.

ADAPTED FROM A QUOTE FROM TERESA OF AVILA, 1515-1582

God of all journeys, we set out now in pilgrimage, leaving aside the clutter and distraction of the world. We walk in the footsteps of many who have trod this pathway and we call on you to be our guide, our companion on the way. We set out now following the call within us to spend time with each other, listening and sharing and giving ourselves to hear one another and our inner selves. We are thankful for all those who will be supporting us along this journey and ask for your blessings on them. In Jesus, Amen

CELTIC PRAYER BOOK FOR PILGRIMAGE

Jesus, forgive my sins. Forgive the sins that I can remember, and also the sins I have forgotten.

Forgive the wrong actions I have committed, and the right actions I have omitted. Forgive the times I have been weak in the face of temptation, and those when I have been stubborn in the face of correction. Forgive the times I have been proud of my own achievements, and those when I have failed to boast of your works. Forgive the harsh judgments I have made of others, and the leniency I have shown to myself. Forgive the lies I have told to others, and the truths I have avoided. Forgive me of the pain I have caused others, and the indulgence I have shown to myself. Jesus have pity on me, and make me whole.

FROM THE *CELTIC PRIMER*

APPENDIX 4

SCRIPTED PRAYERS BY THE AUTHOR

WHILE PASTORING IN GREENWICH, I developed weekly morning and evening prayer cards to accompany certain preaching series. Many from the church body would pray these prayers as a part of their daily pursuit of God. Some learned how to pray spontaneously by starting with these prepared prayers. Over time they became more comfortable speaking out an extemporaneous prayer to the Lord. I have had people pull out a couple dozen of these cards when I visited their homes. They post them on bathroom mirrors or kitchen refrigerators to be prayed for a week at a time and then recycled. These prayers may ignite, launch, or refresh your own prayer apprenticeship.

PRAYERS FOR THE WORK OF THE HOLY SPIRIT IN OUR LIVES

Day 1—Morning Prayer
God, I start this day looking to you for life and purpose. I recognized that you are not far from me since you have called me the temple of the Holy Spirit.

Holy Spirit, as we start the day together, I give you access to every room in this temple. Fill me and use me as a reflection of your presence in this world. I trust you to give me direction and insight throughout the day to do this well. In Jesus' name, Amen.

Day 1—Evening Prayer

Lord, I began this day by acknowledging your indwelling presence in me. I thank you for never being far away, even when I was not attentive to your presence. Holy Spirit, I ask you to release conviction for the actions and attitudes that were outside of your best plan for me. Cleansing breath of God, blow through this temple to make me new again. In Jesus' name, Amen.

Day 2—Morning Prayer

Father, I begin this day in vibrant relationship with you. I can do this because you have pursued me in love. Jesus your victory on the cross and in resurrection, declare "no condemnation" over my life. I am free. Holy Spirit, your promise is to live through me so that your ways would be stronger than the ways of my flesh. I submit God to your work of love, victory, and strength. Fill me anew this day. In Jesus' name, Amen.

Day 2—Evening Prayer

Lord, I began this day aligned to you through Jesus. Your love was my covering. So, I can rest this evening knowing that nothing has come my way except through the filters of your love. Forgive me for the moments when I cooperated more with my fleshly desire than your Spirit's way of life. What is broken, bring healing. What is downcast, bring new life. Again tonight I hide in your love and peace. In Jesus' name, Amen.

Day 3—Morning Prayer

Heavenly Father, you are the giver of all life. Today is a gift from you. I commit my daily activities into your hands. I want to be a good steward of every opportunity—time, talent, treasure. Fill me with your Spirit to be successful. I accept that the people who come my way today are a gift from you. May I see your image in them, emote hope to them, and be a source of help in their journey. In Jesus' name, Amen.

Day 3—Evening Prayer

Father, I give this day back to you as worship. May all good that flowed out of my life bring glory to you. Jesus, I give this day back to you as worship. I stand behind the cross where you redeem my failures. Holy Spirit, I give this day back to you as worship. Please bless the people that I interacted with this day. Lord, I ask you to cover these people and my family under the banner of your peace. In Jesus' name, Amen.

Day 4—Morning Prayer

Holy Spirit, you have opened the eyes of my heart to the love of the Father and called me into relationship with you through the grace of the Lord Jesus Christ. Mysteriously you have made your dwelling place in my inner person. I start this day by asking for a fresh filling. I give you access to every chamber of my heart. Mold me, shape me, fill me, use me. I accept your power and energy for this day. In Jesus, Amen.

Day 4—Evening Prayer

Holy Spirit, you have been my source of life all day long. Thank you for your faithfulness. I ask you to brighten your witness to the people that I touched with word or deed in Jesus's name today. I ask for forgiveness of my sins—cleanse me with your purifying fire. I ask for your peace through the night—a clear witness to my heart that I am hidden in you, as I rest tonight. In Jesus, Amen.

PRAYERS CRAFTED IN COORDINATION WITH THE LORD'S PRAYER

Our Father—Morning Prayer

Heavenly Father, I marvel that you delight in talking with me. I purposefully look for your promised presence in my life today. Jesus, as your disciple, I ask you to teach me how to pray. Holy Spirit, since I do not know how to pray as I ought, I ask you to pray through me this day. God, I am listening for you, and I commit myself to you anew. In Jesus's name, Amen.

Our Father—Evening Prayer

Lord, I look back on this day with thanksgiving. I am grateful for the places where I saw Your presence so clearly. I ask for your forgiveness for the moments where I tuned you out. If you want to speak to me in the night I am listening. I ask for your peace and rest so that I would be renewed in strength and awake with courage for a new day. In Jesus's name, Amen.

Hallowed Be—Morning Prayer

Our Father in heaven, hallowed be your name. Lord, where do I begin to get my mind around this invitation to pray. Hallowed—totally Other, Holy, Magnificent is your name. Yet you give me a familiar approach: daddy, pops, loving father. I do not take this privilege for granted. I come under the shadow of your cover for this day—you are for me, in what shall I be afraid? In Jesus's name, Amen.

Hallowed Be—Evening Prayer

Lord, I started this day by putting myself under your cover. I end it by thanking you in every experience, both good and bad, because you were right there with me. Where I shined in this day, may people see this as a reflection of your glory. Where I did not shine so well, I ask your forgiveness. I come to this moment of rest committing all into your hands and accepting your gift of peace for this night. In Jesus's name, Amen.

Your Kingdom Come—Morning Prayer

Our Father, our King, we intercede for your kingdom to come. We begin this day by cooperating with this movement by asking for your grace and power to do your will. Make us alert and responsive to the places and people that we meet today that are waiting for your mishpat, your justice through restoration. In Jesus, Amen.

Your Kingdom Come—Evening Prayer

Our Father, our King, thank you for allowing us to live under the safety of your rule in this day. Forgive us for the moments when we tried to live in our own way or simply unknowingly veered from your path. We now place ourselves under the canopy of your shalom—to rest well this night. We ask for the same for our neighborhood. In Jesus, Amen.

Give Us—Morning Prayer

Our Father, our Provider, I begin this day by acknowledging you as the Giver of every good and perfect gift. I am grateful for your Provision in my life. I trust you today for all my basic needs. As I have bread available to eat, I want also to be filled with you, the Bread of Life and Living Water. Thus, I ask you to remind me with every drink and every bite of food in the day that you are enough for me. In Jesus, Amen.

Give Us—Evening Prayer

Lord, my Sustainer and Friend, I look on this day with thankfulness. I did not get everything I wanted today, but I still choose contentment. I pray for those who did not even receive the basics today. I pray for the hungry, the thirsty, the cold, and the lonely. I ask you to watch over them and when possible let me serve them in the days to come. Once again, I declare that you are Enough for me. In Jesus, Amen.

Forgive Us—Morning Prayer

Our Father and Holy God, You are perfect in all your ways, yet at the same time merciful and compassionate to us. I begin this day embraced by your steadfast love. Your kindness empowers me to face this dark world in Your Holiness. Fill me up with your Holy Spirit so that I might walk as Jesus. I ask that you would make my life a reflection of your glorious light. In Jesus, Amen.

Forgive Us—Evening Prayer

Master, you have been so good to me this day. Even when I was distracted by the darkness around me, You continued to make Your name Holy in my midst. I confess where I walked outside your way. I know you forgive according to your promises. I choose tonight to forgive those who have wronged me, knowingly or unknowingly. I release them and allow no place for bitter root. I rest in you! In Jesus, Amen.

Deliver Us—Morning Prayer

Our Father, Almighty God, Ancient of Days, the one who sits on the throne. We begin this day not knowing what lies ahead. At the same time, we are at peace because we know you, and more importantly, you know us. You are our Stronghold, Refuge, and Tower of Strength. Since you are for us, who can be against us? We move into this day positioned in Christ's authority to live for his glory. In Jesus, Amen.

Deliver Us—Evening Prayer

Lord, you have kept us this day. For all that went well we are thankful. For whatever was unpleasant we still remain thankful because we did not face it alone. You were with us! Where we gave in to temptation, we now confess to you coming again to your forgiveness and freedom. We look to you as our peace to rest well this night. We hide in you our Stronghold, Refuge, and Tower of Strength. In Jesus, Amen.

Yours is—Morning Prayer

Our Father, yours is the kingdom, and the Power, and the Glory, Forever. So, I begin this day living the overflow of your life in me. May your kingdom come in love and purity today. I ask for a fresh filling of your Holy Spirit for power in my witness. Release joy through my countenance to reflect your glory in this world—shine Jesus! I live fully in the present knowing that my Forever is safe in you. In Jesus, Amen.

Yours is—Evening Prayer

Our Father, yours is the kingdom, and the Power, and the Glory, Forever. So, I end this day fully secure in you. To the broken situations, places and people that I came across today, I ask for your Kingdom, Power and Glory, to bring new life. To those places in my personal life that need transformation, I ask for the same. Forever secure, I can trust you for the immediate. Fill our night with peace. In Jesus, Amen.

GENERAL PRAYERS

Day 1—Morning Prayer

Dear Heavenly Father, today I approach you in prayer because I know that you pursued me first in your love. Thank you for welcoming me into your throne room through Jesus Christ, the Great High Priest. And thank you for giving me your Holy Spirit, who prays through me so that I can just openly talk with you. Today I embrace my role as your ambassador priest in this world. I accept the task of looking actively for people and situations to bring to you in prayer. Open my eyes to your opportunities. In Jesus' name, Amen.

Day 1—Evening Prayer

Dear Lord, I look back on this day with thanksgiving. Everything was gift from you: success, struggle, opportunity, disappointment, joy, and the very breath of life, both in body and spirit. I am alive in Jesus, thank you! I commit to you all the places of prayer in this day. I trust you for the outcome of each, even if it is not exactly what I wanted. Your ways are higher than my ways. Under Jesus, now I entrust myself to you for renewing rest. In Jesus' name, Amen

Day 2—Morning Prayer
Almighty God, who reveals in fire and with word, Abba Father, who loves me without condition, I choose to enter this day embracing the mystery of coming to you, the great I AM, God who is transcendent and yet near. You are an awesome God, to be worshipped and obeyed. You are a loving God, to be trusted and embraced. I enter this day looking for your manifest presence in the mundane details. Where you call I will follow. By your Spirit, open my eyes to my burning bushes. In Jesus' name, Amen.

Day 2—Evening Prayer
Great I AM, liberator of the people of God through the generations, and my liberator today. You have been with me all day long, even when I missed your presence. Thank you! As I come to the end of the day, I ask that the same fire that called to Moses would burn away my sin. I pray that the same Spirit that was in the fire, would surround me and my family, with comfort, rest, and quietness this night. I feel safe going to sleep as I belong to you. In Jesus' name, Amen.

Day 3—Morning Prayer
Dear Heavenly Father, Father of Abraham, Isaac, and Jacob, and my Abba Father.
Today you ordained all types of experiences and encounters for me. Since they are your assignments, I choose to trust you. I need the faith of my spiritual ancestors to attack the challenges

of this day. I ask boldly that your presence would be manifest in these moments. I want to live as an intercessor of blessing for the people that I meet along the way. Release faith and boldness in my approach of you. In Jesus' name, Amen.

Day 3—Evening Prayer

Dear Heavenly Father, I give back to you all the challenges of this day. You have been my companion and strength to arrive at this moment. I thank you for every place where your presence was obvious and the places where you were active, but I missed your presence. For the situations that did not turn out as I desired or asked, I ask for your intervention once again. Hear my prayer! I choose to ask in boldness, in the pattern of Jesus, "your will be done!"
In Jesus' name, Amen.

Day 4—Morning Prayer

Lord,
I do not fear this day, for you are with me
Wherever I might go.
Your light shines ahead; your footsteps lead the way.
I do not fear this day for your word will be my guide.
Your strength will sustain me, your love revive me,
this day and all days,
I do not fear this day, for you are with me.
Amen

Day 4—Evening Prayer

Eternal God, ruler of all creation,
You have allowed me to reach this hour.

Forgive the sins I have committed this day by word, deed or thought.
If I have wounded a soul today, Lord forgive me.
If words I have said caused misery, Lord forgive me.
Grant that I might rise from sleep to glorify you my entire lifetime,
For Yours is the kingdom and the power and the glory forever.
Amen

Prayers on Pilgrimage

Lord of the journey, I have lost my way.
Vision for the finish line is dim.
Energy for the run is low.
I have lost step with your Spirit.
My only hope in finishing well is
found in you. So I recommit to the race that
you have marked out for me. I throw off
every weight and the sin that slows me down.
I run, struggling with your energy that so powerfully works in me.
With each step, Lord, quicken my pace by your Spirit.

Father, where will the road take me today?
I choose your way.
In step with your Spirit my footing is sure.
In step with Jesus my arrival secure.
Amen.

Bless to me, O God,
The earth beneath my feet.
Bless to me, O God,
The path where I go.

I in Thy path, O God,
Thou, O God, in my step.

Today, the journey is pleasurable.
Tomorrow offers no guarantees.
May I be as content in both days.
Thank you Lord for your presence in good and bad days.
While I journey today, may I be a source of life for those
whose path is less pleasant.

God, bless the pathway of this day.
By your Spirit, bless the people I meet along the way.
By your Son, invite the wanderers back to His Way.
By your Fatherly love, keep me sure in your own path, even when
the way is rough.
I am blessed to walk with you. Make me a blessing to those who
walk with me.

Lord, we join a long train of pilgrims who sought your Way.
Our early faith-filled fathers and mothers were exiles on the
earth, moving to a better city. Our Jewish ancestors ascended
to Zion to meet you in worship and sacrifice. We continue the
journey as they did not receive what was promised. We throw off
everything and the sin that weighs us down and set out on the
pilgrimage that you have marked out before us, looking to Jesus,
our true Way-maker. May each step we take in training be an
act of worship as we draw closer to you each day in the light of
your promise: "draw close to me and I will draw close to you."
In the name of Jesus, whose pilgrimage crossed the boundaries of
the divine into human frailty, that we might find abundance
in this life and resurrection into the next. Amen.

BIBLIOGRAPHY

Anderson, Neil. *The Prayers of Jesus*, Zondervan, 2007.

Barclay, William. *The Mind of Jesus*, SCM Press Ltd., 1976.

Barnes, M. Craig. *Yearning*, InterVarsity Press, 1991.

Barth, Karl. *Prayer*, Westminster John Knox Press, 2002.

Batterson, Mark. *All In: You Are One Decision Away From a Totally Different Life*, Zondervan, 2013.

Bevere, John. *The Bait of Satan*. Charisma House, 2014

Bonhoeffer, Dietrich. *The Cost of Discipleship*, Holman Reference, 2017.

Bonhoeffer, Dietrich. *The Bonhoeffer Reader*, edited by Clifford Green and Michael Dejonge, Fortress Press, 2013.

Bounds, E.M. "God Shapes the World Through Prayer," *Purpose in Prayer*. Available at HeraldOfHisComing.com, August 2013 issue.

Boyle, Gregory. *Barking to the Choir*, Simon & Shuster, 2017.

Bunyan, John. *The Poetry of John Bunyan*, Vol I., Portable Poetry, 2017.

Burr, Richard. *Developing Your Secret Closet of Prayer*, Wingspread, 2008.

Buttrick, George Arthur (Ed.). *The Interpreter's Dictionary of the Bible*, Vol. 3, Abingdon Press, 1962.

Coakley, Sarah. *Dom John Chapman, O.S.B. (1865–1933)*, The Way, 1990. Available at TheWay.org.uk

Comer, John Mark. *God has a Name*, Zondervan, 2017.

Comfort, Philip W., and Wendell C. Hawley. *Opening John's Gospel and Epistles*, Tyndale House Publishers., 2009.

Cosper, Mike. *Recapturing the Wonder*, InterVarsity Press, 2017.

Duewel, Wesley. *Touch the World through Prayer*, Zondervan, 1986.

Duewel, Wesley. "How to Use God's Word for a Vibrant Prayer Life," August 23, 2013. Available at FaithGateway.com

Finney, Charles G. "Lecture VIII: Meetings for Prayer," *Lectures on the Revival of Religion*, 1868. Available at GospelTruth.net

Foster, Richard. *Prayer*, Harper Collins, 1992.

Frangipane, Francis. *The Stronghold of God*, Charisma House, 1998.

Graham, Franklin. *Billy Graham in Quotes*, Thomas Nelson, 2011.

Hurnard, Hannah. *God's Transmitters*, Mass Market Paperback, 1976.

Hutchinson, Gloria, *Six Ways to Pray from Six Great Saints*, Franciscan Media, 2015.

Bromiley, Geoffrey, ed. *The International Standard Bible Encyclopedia*, Vol 3, Erdmans, 1986.

Johnson, Bill. *When Heaven Invades Earth*, Destiny Image Publishers, 2003.

Kant, Immanuel. "Religion" in *Lectures on Ethics*, 1775–1780. Translated by Lewis Infield, Methuen, 1930.

Kraft, Charles. *Communication Theory for Christian Witness*, Orbis, 1995.

à Kempis, Thomas. *The Inner Life*, Penguins Books, 1952.

Laubach, Frank *Letters by a Modern Mystic*, Purposeful Design Publications, 2007.

Lawrence, Brother. *The Practice of the Presence of God*, Doubleday, 1977.

Lewis, C.S. *Yours, Jack*, HarperOne, 2009.

Lewis, C.S. *Letters to Malcolm: Chiefly on Prayer*, Harcourt, Brace and World, 1963.

Lucado, Max. *When God Whispers Your Name*, Thomas Nelson, 2011.

MacDonald, George. "Man's Difficulty Concerning Prayer," *Unspoken Sermons*. Available at The Literature Network, http://www.online–literature.com.

Marx, Karl. *A Contribution to the Critique of Hegel's Philosophy of Right*, 1843. Translation by Annette Jolin and Joseph O'Malley, Cambridge University Press, 1970.

Merton, Thomas. *Conjectures of a Guilty Bystander*, Image Press, 1968.

Metaxas, Eric. *Bonhoeffer: Pastor, Martyr, Prophet, Spy*, Thomas Nelson, 2011.

Miller, Calvin. *The Path of Celtic Prayer*, IVP Books, 2012.

Miller, Paul E. *A Praying Life*, Navpress, 2017.

Murray, Andrew. *Lord Teach Us to Pray*, Gideon House Books, 2016.

Murray, Andrew. *Waiting on God*, 1896. Reprinted by Infinity, 2015.

Murray, Andrew. *With Christ in the School of Prayer*, Baker Books, 1953.

Nouwen, Henri. *Discernment: Reading the Signs of Daily Life*, Image Press, 2013.

Paul, Greg. *Close Enough to Hear God Breathe*, Thomas Nelson, 2011.

Payne, Leanne. *Listening Prayer*, Baker Books, 1994.

Peterson, Eugene. *A Long Obedience in the Same Direction*, InterVarsity Press, 2009.

Peterson, Eugene. *First and Second Samuel*. Westminster John Knox Press.1999.

Pierson, A.T. *The New Acts of the Apostles*, The Baker &Taylor Co., 1894.

Piper, John. "We Have Not Because We Ask Not," December 28, 1981. Available at desiringGod.org.

Piper, John. *A Hunger for God*, Crossway, 2013.

Piper, John. *Desiring God*, Multnomah, 2011.

Piper, John. *The Pleasures of God,* Multnomah, 2012.

Piper, John. *When I Don't Desire God*, Crossway Books, 2004.

Pratt, Lonni Collins, and Fr. Daniel Homan, O.S.B. *The Benedict Way*, Loyola Press, 2000.

Prime, Derek and Alistair Begg. *On Being a Pastor*, Moody Press, 2013.

Rohr, Richard. *Everything Belongs*, Crossroad Publishing Company, 2003.

Romanov, Sergei. "Tolstoy and the Sign of the Cross," December 28, 2012. Available at Pravmir.com.

Rutledge, Fleming. *Advent*, Eerdmans, 2018.

Schnabel, Eckhard. *Acts*, Zondervan, 2012.

Sheets, Dutch. *Intercessory Prayer*, Bethany House Publishers, 2006.

Sorge, Bob *Secrets of the Secret Place*, Oasis House, 2013.

Spurgeon, Charles H. *Spurgeon on Prayer: How to Converse with God*, Bridge–Logos, 2009.

Spurgeon, Charles H. "Prayer Certified of Success," *Spurgeon's Sermons*, Vol. 19, delivered January 19, 1873. Available at Christian Classics Ethereal Library, www.ccel.org.

Tan, Siang–Yang, and Douglas Gregg. *Disciplines of the Holy Spirit*, Zondervan, 1997.

Taylor, Hudson. *Hudson Taylor's Spiritual Secret*, Mass Market Paperback, 1955.

Towns, Elmer. *Fasting for Spiritual Breakthrough*, Bethany House Publishers, 1996.

Tozer, A.W. *The Pursuit of God,* Christian Publications, 1948.

Tutu, Desmond. *God has a Dream*, Ebury Publishing, 2004.

Wagner, Peter. *Confronting the Powers*, Destiny Image Publishers, 1996.

Wagner, Peter. *Prayer Shield*, Chosen Books, 1992.

Willard, Dallas. *The Divine Conspiracy*, HarperOne, 2009.

Yaconelli, Michael. *Messy Spirituality*, Zondervan, 2002.

Yancey, Philip. *Prayer*, Zondervan, 2006.

Opposition! It is inevitable in any worthwhile pursuit. Jesus even promised challenge in the faith journey, "In the world you will have tribulation. But take heart; I have overcome the world" (John 16:33). There is a bit of a reflex in us when hearing these words from Jesus—you have overcome but what about me. It does not always feel like I am overcoming. Davis presents the case that one key aspect of being an overcomer for the Christ follower is the notion of spiritual authority. Living in a world that is rooted in power, Christ followers are challenged daily by powers that seek to interrupt or trample their success in the journey through Christ—the world and the kingdom of darkness. Davis believes that while followers receive empowerment from the Holy Spirit, this power is only fully operational as they function out of their God-given authority. As believers, everything they need is at their disposal. However, they must actively appropriate their authority, both in attitude and in action. Davis provides a biblical theology of authority and real life examples of how he and others have embraced their spiritual authority to advance the kingdom of God. In essence, it is a manual for overcoming spiritual opposition in everyday life.

ISBN 9780825307805 Paperback $14.95

EL CRISTIANO ATREVIDO

¡Oposición! Es inevitable en cualquier búsqueda que vale la pena. Jesús incluso prometió desafío en el camino de la fe, "En el mundo tendréis aflicción; pero confiad, yo he vencido al mundo." (Juan 16:33). Nos asombramos un poco al escuchar estas palabras de Jesús—has vencido, pero ¿y yo qué?. No siempre se siente como si yo estuviera venciendo.Davis explica que un aspecto clave de ser un vencedor para el seguidor de Cristo es la noción de autoridad espiritual. Viviendo en un mundo que está arraigado en el poder, los seguidores de Cristo son desafiados diariamente por los poderes que buscan interrumpir o pisotear su éxito en el caminar con Cristo—el mundo y el reino de las tinieblas. Davis cree que aunque los seguidores reciben el empoderamiento del Espíritu Santo, este poder sólo es plenamente operativo mientras que actúen bajo su autoridad dada por Dios. Como creyente, todo lo que necesitan está a su disposición. Sin embargo, deben activamente apropiarse de su autoridad, tanto en actitud como en acción. Davis proporciona una teología bíblica de la autoridad y ejemplos de la vida real de cómo él y otros han aceptado su autoridad espiritual para avanzar el reino de Dios. En esencia es un manual para superar la oposición espiritual en la vida cotidiana.

ISBN 9780825308765 Paperback $14.95

JONAH AND ME

There is an inherent desire in all of us to know that our lives really matter. We were created to flourish. Unfortunately, many of the models or aspirations of flourishing from our culture are limiting. This is because they are disconnected from God's original design for us. We flourish most when we find our lives in the overflow of what God is doing in this world.God is a missionary God. Throughout the Scriptures, God again and again, invites his people to be on mission with him. The story of Jonah in the Hebrew scriptures is one of God's most graphic callings. It is a midcourse correction for the children of God. It is also an invitation to all of us to ask if we are on mission with God. After exploring the story of Jonah, *Jonah and Me*, will unfold a biblical theology of mission. Beginning in Genesis and moving through Revelation, using the larger themes of being chosen, called, and commissioned, we will see how God has been inviting his children to be on mission with him throughout the ages. Finally, the book will offer suggestions on how to discover, rediscover, or simply reenergize in your life mission.

ISBN 9780825308758 Paperback $14.95